Success Stories

By Jessica Roberts

Using Video Stories to Connect, Communicate, and Create True Success With Your Students

Cover Design By Brittanie Stumpp

ISBN: 1-4392-0785-2

To order additional copies, please contact us. BookSurge Publishing
www.booksurge.com

1-866-308-6235 orders@booksurge.com

Table of Contents

Foreword: What the Research Says about Video Stories

The research in support of Video Modeling and Video Self Modeling (VSM) is some of the strongest we have for interventions for students on the autism spectrum. A Meta-Analysis conducted by Scott Bellini and Jennifer Akullian published in *The Exceptional Child Journal* Spring 2007 reported on the effects twenty-three single subject design studies. Some of the findings are:

- o Skills acquired through video modeling and VSM generalize to other persons and settings
- o Skills acquired through video modeling and VSM maintain for months following the intervention
- o Video modeling and VSM have been shown to be effective for students with Significant Cognitive Disabilities
- o The video segments can be short. The average length of the videos was three minutes.

Video modeling and VSM have been shown to be effective in teaching:

- o Behavioral Functioning
    - o Reducing Problem Behaviors
    - o On Task Behaviors
- o Social –Communication Skills
    - o Conversational Skills
    - o Play Skills
    - o Social Initiations
    - o Social Responses
- o Functional Skills
    - o Purchasing Behaviors
    - o Hygiene
    - o Other Self Help Skills

The only pre-requisite skill is that students must be willing and able to attend to the video. Even if the student has vision problems, they may still be very attentive to the sound of their voice in the movies.

Video self-modeling and Video Stories work well because they are visual strategies which are well adapted to teach students whose visual processing abilities exceed their language processing abilities. Video Stories focus the child's attention on relevant and significant stimuli in the environment, thereby assuring that they are learning what the teacher is intending to teach in the lesson. Perhaps most importantly, Video Stories are highly motivating. Watching videos, especially when the students and their friends are the movie stars, is an enjoyable activity for many students. The students may be having so much fun, they do not realize they are learning important skills.

Jessica Roberts is part of the generation that grew up with digital technology, so it was natural for her to incorporate Video Stories into her instruction of students with significant disabilities. Additionally, being a brilliant teacher, she shares her understanding in a step-by-step comprehensible fashion for those of us who are DSL (digital as a second language). Jessica has taken the research-based strategy of video self modeling and extended its implementation to support interventions in all areas of service for her students.

At the Utah Personnel Development Center, we have worked with Jessica to encourage the use of Video Self Modeling for students with autism and significant disabilities throughout the state, and we are seeing other teachers replicate her success. In this book, Jessica and her students will show you how to bring the fun back into teaching as you watch your own students learn to teach themselves to succeed.

Catherine Longstroth
Utah Personnel Development Center
Autism and Significant Disabilities Specialist

Video Stories: An Introduction

See it. Do it. Teach it.

"See it. Do it. Teach it." is an educational philosophy practiced in the medical field as well as in many effective classrooms. Video Stories provide a framework for implementing that sort of active learning environment in your classroom or your home. Video Stories not only help your students see clearly what they need to do, and complete the skill successfully, but they also give the students the opportunity to see themselves achieving their goals, thereby securing their success.

With Video Stories, the students see themselves accomplishing something, and then there's no question about it. They know they can do it. They feel entirely competent. They exude self-efficacy – the belief in their own ability to succeed. They may begin to initiate their new skills right away, and learn from each successful attempt. They gain a powerful sense of confidence, thinking along the lines of "If I can do that, what else can I do?"

Video Stories are movies or PowerPoint slideshows that incorporate video clips of your students engaging in a desired skill with all the essential information needed to understand that skill. The essential information can be included with words, symbols, or narration.

Children learn by doing. Adults learn by doing, too. With the help of this guidebook, you will learn how to create Video Stories by actually making your own. You can read the visual step-by-step directions and watch the examples and video tutorials on the website. However, the real learning will occur when you take a deep breath, put what you've seen into practice, and begin your own Video Story.

A Little Pep Talk

Do you ever wish you had a magic wand that could get your students' attention? (And I don't mean by whacking them with it.) Do you feel the need for a translator when your students stare blankly at you or miss something you've told them a hundred times? Do you sometimes get stuck just trying to survive through another day of the same old problems, too worn out to accomplish any real change?

We all have days like that. However, Video Stories can help in each of those areas. This powerful teaching tool can help you connect with your students, communicate clearly and effectively what they need to know, and create true Success Stories out of seemingly insurmountable obstacles.

With camera in hand, you can hold your students' attention and interest, engage them to actively listen and learn, and capture the precise moment in which the students complete a skill successfully. Once the students see themselves as the "movie stars," they may begin to imitate the video and initiate their new skills in various settings. Almost immediately! We don't get to use the word "immediately" very often in special education, so it may infuse some intense excitement and momentum into your instruction. You may start to refer to your camera as a magic wand.

Nearly any concept you need to teach can be presented in the format of a Video Story. In my classroom, we've created Video Stories about why to resist eating food off of the cafeteria floor as well as how to measure density. These stories can be as diverse as the students they are created for, and yet each story is formed from the same simple procedures: analyzing the task into small accessible steps and providing essential information with the intense visual support of video self modeling.

This guidebook provides you with easy to follow visual instructions to lead you through the process of creating your Video Stories. Whether you use the PowerPoint 2003, PowerPoint 2007, Windows Movie Maker, or iMovie programs, you will find all the essential information you'll need, as well as some helpful visual support, including pictures of the computer screen at each step. To watch video tutorials of my computer screen as I walk you through each step, visit my website at www.wsdstaff.net/~jroberts and click on Success Story Instructions.

If traditional methods fail to reach your students, Video Stories can teach:

Appropriate Behavior, Schedules/Routines, Language Development, Classroom Expectations, Social Skills, Independent Living Skills, Any Academic Concept, & much more!

This guide will help you:

- **CONNECT** – Reach your students. Motivate them to listen. Engage them to actively participate and learn. Capture their attention and their moments of success with your camera.

- **COMMUNICATE** – Clarify nearly any skill or subject matter into small accessible steps your students can accomplish. Relate the essential information in a format your students can understand, use, and remember.

- **CREATE** – Create sincere, dramatic, positive change. Compose essential information and the video clips of your student into a multimedia Video Story. Present the Video Story with big fanfare and celebration. Share their success with family and friends on CDs or DVDs.

Not Just for Special Education

Video Stories can be individualized to the issues your students face or the concepts they need to learn, whether the students are typically functioning or otherwise. Though the stories in this book describe ways I've used Video Stories in my Special Needs classroom, this research-validated teaching strategy can be incorporated into the structure of a general education classroom or home environment. Parents may find the concept of using home movies to create educational Video Stories an enjoyable and effective way to teach their children many important skills.

Video Stories can be shared between home and school, in order to develop a common language and understanding of the steps to a skill, and an increased success in generalizing the skill. Likewise, they enable the students to synthesize information and demonstrate their understanding. Perhaps most importantly, Video Stories establish a connection between you and your students, motivating and engaging even the hard to reach students to become personally involved in the learning process.

As you read this guidebook, I hope you will be able to transfer these thoughts and examples to your own situation and come up with your own ideas about how to use Video Stories with the child or children in your life.

What you will Need

If you do not have access to some of these items, either at home or at school, don't fret. You have several options. You could convince your administration, or spouse, or state office of education to provide the tools you need, by discussing the many wonderful ways in which you will use this teaching strategy. Or you could buy the items yourself. Even video camcorders are surprisingly affordable now. (Some are only $100!)

These are the items you will *need* to create Video Stories.
- Video Camcorder.
- Computer with either Windows Movie Maker, PowerPoint 2003, PowerPoint 2007, or iMovie installed.
- Fire Wire or Video USB cable to send video to your computer.

These are the items you may *want* to create Video Stories.
- LCD Screen Projector to increase student participation
- Laser Pointer to increase student participation

If you don't have access to a projector or laser pointer, the students can still participate by gathering around the computer.

How do you find the Time?

What if I were to tell you that you don't have to do this after school? You should know that this teaching strategy is intended to be implemented and completed right there in the classroom as part of the lesson. So much of a teacher's time is wasted on non-teaching activities, like paperwork and meetings. Video Stories are essentially about teaching. I do most, if not all, of the work for each Video Story as I'm teaching, with my students actively participating in each part of the process.

If you're anything like me you have a magical To-Do List, something like *The Never-Ending Story*. Video Stories are the most enjoyable thing on my list, as well as the most effective use of my time. So Video Stories work their way up to the top of the list. I will describe how I schedule and implement this strategy in my classroom, and you can transfer the ideas to the needs of your students and the structure of your situation.

Most of the time, I have the students in a small group. I have a class period scheduled into the day to work on Video Stories related to the needs of my kids, such as social skills or language development. I call the class "Video Stories" or "Movie Makers," but of course, you can call it whatever you want. If you have large groups of more than ten in your class, I would encourage you to focus on six to ten students at a time, and arrange a separate activity for the others. With some of the more challenging students, I create their Video Stories while I'm working one on one with them, using their video stories to teach the skills they need to increase their tolerance for group settings and eventually participate in the larger group.

I introduce the new concept or skill by showing the small accessible steps that make up the larger skill. Sometimes my students and I brainstorm together to come up with these basic steps. My students practice the skill by acting out and recording each step of the skill, with prompting as necessary. When we capture the video from the camcorder to the computer, we are editing at the same time. We cut out the prompts as much as possible, so it looks like the student has completed that step successfully and independently. The students have the opportunity to see themselves several times as we bring the video clip to the computer, as a projector displays the computer screen for the whole group to see. When the video includes some mischievousness or some inappropriate behaviors, I edit that part of the video on my own, so the students aren't tempted to imitate the mischief. But otherwise, even the editing can quickly be done in the classroom with your students actively participating.

Then the students take turns with a laser pointing to the buttons on the projected computer screen and helping me insert the videos and text into the story.

If the student has trouble figuring out where to point the laser, I can provide assistance just by nonchalantly pointing toward the correct place with my mouse. My students love the laser and are thoroughly engaged in figuring out these cool computer programs and creating their own Video Stories. The students also brainstorm with me to come up with the words to put on each page, "helping" me with spelling and sentence structure. They take turns reading the words on each page before we watch the video clip. So, the recording, editing, creating, and showing of the Video Story all become important components of the lesson.

Most of my students know how to insert pictures, videos, and even animations into PowerPoint. They also can make sophisticated Video Stories with music, text, pictures and video clips in Windows Movie Maker. You can do it, too!

But Technology is Terrifying!

I'm guessing some of you are a little intimidated by the technological aspect of Video Stories. Really, it's not too hard. It does not require manual labor or technical expertise. It's likely you won't even break a sweat. These cameras and computer programs are built to do exactly what you want them to do. A click of a button (or a couple buttons) and Voila! I will show you exactly which buttons to push. Each button you need to click on will be clearly underlined, and you'll see pictures at each step. This guidebook will be your one-stop resource for simplified information on how to create a Video Story in Windows Movie Maker, PowerPoint, or iMovie. We start with how to open the program, and yet by the end you will know how to add animation and music to your Video Stories. You'll also find video tutorials on each step of the process at my website – www.wsdstaff.net/~jroberts.

I should maybe warn you that you might enjoy this after a while. You might find yourself getting excited about all kinds of fun and fabulous projects with your videos and pictures, both at work and at home. As an extra benefit, once you learn how to create a Video Story, you'll also be quite familiar with the tools of digital scrapbooking and home movie editing. The technological things that you learn through this process can be extended to many other programs and increase your computer competency. The functions you'll learn in PowerPoint work just the same in other Windows programs, like Microsoft Word. Also, if you're using an Apple computer, as you maneuver through iMovie, you'll become connected to a great network of programs like iPhoto, iTunes, iDVD, and iWeb. If you run into some obstacles, don't give up. You can find assistance at the online support for each program, the built-in help function for each program, or with your friendly, neighborhood computer guy.

Don't sell yourself short. This is not nearly as hard as most of the other incredibly hard things you do throughout the day. Give it a try!

A Bit of Research

Since Video Stories are a combination of the two research-validated strategies of social stories and video self-modeling, there is a wealth of information supporting its implementation. Research has shown that both social stories and video modeling have stood out from other instructional methods as effective ways of teaching these important skills to students with autism and significant disabilities.

Social stories have been widely used with students with autism to substantially increase communication skills (Soenksen & Alper, 2006), social interaction (Barry & Burlew, 2004), and appropriate behavior (Crozier & Tincani, 2005). In a synthesis of the research regarding social stories, Sansosti, Powell-Smith and Kincaid (2004) concluded that social stories can serve as a positive behavior support intervention to internalize and generalize necessary skills. Each of the studies reviewed in the synthesis showed social story interventions as an effective way to improve a variety of skills in students with autism at different age and functioning levels (Sansosti et al., 2004).

Video modeling has also proven to be a valuable strategy for teaching, maintaining, and generalizing these important skills, especially for students with autism (Bellini & Akullian, 2007). Video modeling has proven in many empirical studies to be a powerful teaching tool for a variety of different skills, including language skills such as asking and answering questions (Wert & Neisworth, 2003), social skills such as recognizing basic emotions (Corbett, 2003), and behavior skills like refraining from pushing others (Buggey, 2005).

Now that we know that research supports the use of Video Stories in the classroom, we can start to have some fun.

Connect

Reach

Let me tell you how I began the process of making Video Stories in my classroom. I had a student who presented himself more like a bear than a boy. Derek was much bigger than me, and he used his size to assert his authority. He had very limited speech and a diagnosis of severe autism. When he was frustrated or when he was asked to do his school work, he often put on a dramatic and dangerous show of his power. He would charge right through us, knocking over desks, wheelchairs, and desperate adults,

swinging his arms wildly as he made his exit. We had tried everything that the behavior specialists suggested, and yet each day our classroom was like the frontlines of a battlefield, and both sides were losing.

After several months of interfering with Derek's personal agenda and facing disastrous consequences, I was completely worn out, both physically and emotionally. Quitting seemed like the most plausible option. A fellow teacher had talked with me about social stories, and yet it seemed that we could not get Derek to do anything he did not already want to do. And reading was not something he wanted to do.

Then, one day while I was taking pictures of my students, I cautiously asked Derek if I could take his picture. Immediately, he snapped out of his own world and into mine. He cocked his head to the side, opened his eyes wide, and through a goofy grin said, "Cheese!" Then, he wanted to see the picture. I showed it to him on the LCD screen of the camera and he laughed. I laughed with him.

From that moment on, I knew I had a way to reach him. We had a powerful connection. He would do anything I asked as long as I would take his picture. I took pictures of him doing everything including waiting, working, washing his hands, and walking past food on the cafeteria floor. We made PowerPoint stories with his pictures and wrote sentences on each page. He loved watching his slideshows on the computer and got excited about reading his stories. He quickly learned how to type the sentences from a model and insert his pictures into PowerPoint. He recorded his own voice reading each page. It may sound narcissistic, but he couldn't get enough of himself.

Within a few weeks, Derek's aggressive episodes dropped dramatically. The outbursts went from several times a day to only several a year. The amount of work and cooperation we were able to get from him increased exponentially at the same time. We could now challenge him and engage him. We could actually teach him and he continually amazed us with the amount he was able to learn and remember. Behaving like a bear was just a defensive front, and there was an incredibly charming, bright, and beautiful boy underneath who we could begin to get to know.

Another student gave us a run for our money, literally. Erik was a runner and a super strong-willed, independent thinker (to put it nicely). Even if he really wanted to do what we were asking him to do, he would refuse just because we had asked him. He was in control and no amount of persuasion could convince him to cooperate. We had all the latest behavior interventions and reinforcers in our repertoire, but they didn't work. He would do his own thing in his own time, and anything else was impossible. Sound familiar?

Erik liked to run outside and conduct an extremely detailed inspection of all the sprinkler heads around the school. One day, at lunch time, after an entire morning of psychologically draining and completely ineffective attempts at enticing him indoors, he said, "No pennies! No smiles! Just Go Away!" I found the camera, turned the LCD screen so that he could see himself, and said, "We get to make a movie today."

Immediately, he turned and the defiant look on his face melted away; he stared at himself in the camera with a sideways, satisfied smile like a model in a magazine, and walked with me into the classroom. The principal and the other teachers, who were watching, kept repeating the word "magic" as they talked about it throughout the day.

The magic of the camera hasn't worn off yet. In fact, when I ask Erik to do something difficult, he often says, "Camera, please." He also can't get enough of himself, and has made remarkable, even miraculous, improvements in behavior, communication, and social skills through the process of making and watching his Video Stories.

I know many of you face similar challenges with students who are almost impossible to reach. There's so much you need to teach them, but you can't get them to listen. You want to establish a connection, but some of these students have developed a tough protective layer that keeps out intruders and protects their own inner world with its personal plans and comfortable peace. These students may have had overwhelming or confusing experiences dealing with others in the past, and have now created a sort of defense mechanism to maintain personal control. For some students, the camera can become an ambassador into their highly guarded solitary world, and then a messenger drawing out the person behind that shell, in pictures and videos, connecting their world to our own.

Motivate

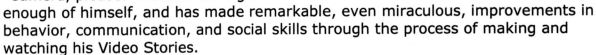

Many children, whether typically-developing or otherwise, are highly motivated by video and computer. Quite a few of your students can recite entire parts of a movie word for word. Why not make a movie of them saying and doing the things they need to say and do? The students themselves become the stars. Then they can recite important and useful information and expand it to real life situations.

"By working from the child's specific interests, you play to that child's strengths – his greatest chance to be motivated and succeed at whatever the task."

- Bryna Siegel, Ph.D.
Helping Children with Autism Learn

You can also intensify the motivation by creating stories that incorporate their particular interests. All children, especially those on the autism spectrum have specific interests that can be incorporated into a Video Story to capture their attention. For example, when I couldn't entice Erik to read his phonics passages, I took pictures of him holding Thomas the Train in various places and then made a Video Story called "The adventures of Thomas the Train." He was excited to read this story and he was actively learning to read important place names in the school such as "office" and "library," as well as common prepositional phrases like "over, under, near, and beside." He was also learning to walk with the teacher to the different places he would need to go during the day.

Perhaps most importantly, Erik was learning how pleasant and beneficial it could be to cooperate and follow directions, something he had not given himself the chance to learn before. We made another story in which Thomas does his work at certain times like a train schedule. We had the student pose with Thomas and a clock while he was doing each task of the day. The story read, "At 7:50, Thomas and Erik do word sorts." By adjusting our curriculum to incorporate the things that motivate our students, we are not only able to teach them more effectively, but we are also able to teach them that learning is fun.

> "If you're having fun, you might learn something by accident."
>
> -Andrea Harris

Engage

As I mentioned before, children learn by doing. Adults learn by doing too, for that matter. If we are actively engaged and interested in the lesson, we will be more likely to remember, implement, and generalize the skills being taught. We all learn better when given the opportunity to participate. We are much more alert and involved than if we were simply expected to watch.

Likewise, you will learn how to create Video Stories by actually making one. You can read about video modeling; you can look at the pictures on the step by step directions; you can watch my Video Stories and think, "Oh, How Cute!" But then, at some point, you will take a deep breath and begin your own Video Story. Once you *do* it, you will *know how to do it*. If you can complete a task successfully, provided with the necessary supports, it brings a new sense of accomplishment or confidence that does not come by reading or watching.

Video Stories actively engage the students by having them act out each part of a process or achieve each step toward a goal. Teaching is more productive if the learners are asked to produce something. Even in academic subjects that are traditionally considered a spectator sport, it is more conducive to long term memory and in-depth understanding to get the students to perform a skill pertaining to the concept, rather than recite answers to test questions. Students can *do* science by conducting experiments, *do* social studies by creating travel guides or news programs, and *do* math by acting out word problems. Likewise, students learn to share by sharing, and the video component of Video Stories helps students who are otherwise not inclined to share become motivated to do so. Video Stories not only motivate and enable the students to accomplish a goal, but then offer the students the opportunity to relish in their accomplishment by watching their slideshows and movies and sharing them with others.

Communicate

Clear Communication

True communication involves presenting the information in a way the other person can understand. True teaching involves presenting the information in a way the students can learn. Video Stories provide a format for presenting information with visual and verbal supports, enabling the students to participate, understand, and learn.

It is important to simplify complex skills or concepts into small, accessible steps that the student can understand and accomplish. It probably won't work to turn your camera on and say, "Do something amazing." (Although that has happened once or twice.) You will need to clarify *how* to do the skill you are trying to teach with step-by-step tasks that the student can either complete independently or learn to complete with visual, verbal, or physical prompts. If the student needs supports or prompts to accomplish a step, do not get discouraged. It is still worthwhile to teach. When you capture the video, you can edit out the prompts as much as possible, and the student will see himself completing the step independently.

Sometimes analyzing each of your desired goals into discrete steps takes a little brainstorming. It helps me to visualize the process like a comic book or a video in slow motion and "freeze-frame" the sequence at each different action. Others of you may prefer writing the steps down like directions in a recipe. Sometimes my students investigate the concept with me and help me evaluate what steps need to be included in what sequence.

Visual Communication

Words

Many of you have tried to learn a second language. Maybe some of you are gifted in that area, but for most of us it is a struggle. I remember going to Spain. I had studied the language for a long time. In a crowded train station I asked directions to the Prado Museum and I felt all proud of myself for getting the words out correctly. But then he answered me. I was struck by a flood of language that I could not understand. All the words seemed connected. I stared at him blankly for a while, and then I asked him to write it down. When I saw where one word ended and another began, I understood.

Many students with autism, attention deficits, or other challenges need the visual support of the written word in the same way. They may have extreme difficulty processing verbal language. Students with autism can often read written words before they can understand verbal speech, and they can often write before they can speak. This occurs because written language is visual and permanent. It doesn't get jumbled around like speech. One of my students who was diagnosed with severe, nonverbal autism did not communicate at all until 4th grade, when he wrote "Car, Keys, McDonalds, Chicken Sandwich" on a piece of paper and handed it to his mother. Spelled correctly and everything!

Do not underestimate your students because they don't seem to understand you or aren't able to respond. Instead, continue to look for ways to present the information so they can comprehend and discover new ways they can participate. It is truly amazing how much they are able to learn when we teach in a way that includes and engages them.

Pictures

A picture is worth a thousand words. I think it's safe to say that a picture is worth a million words when you are dealing with students who have autism or other challenges. Often I see teachers wasting their breath, their time, and their energy saying a million words to a student who has trouble processing verbal language. For these students, it is just as if you are speaking in a foreign language, and repeating your message more emphatically does not increase the level of understanding.

When you travel in a foreign country, you are grateful for any pictures on signs or menus to help you get through the day. When you are reading instructions that are unfamiliar or technical, you welcome and gravitate toward any pictures on the page. For the same reason, I have included pictures and video in this instructional guide, showing each step of the process. Remember your students need it even more than you do.

Many of you have had students who surprise you again and again with a fascinating ability to remember details that are presented visually, like calendar dates, another student's schedule, or entire commercials. Many students with autism and other processing challenges have an amazing visual memory. What if we could extend that skill to remember things that are essential for them to remember? We can. That's what I get excited about. We can access their visual strengths and make the most of it in their instruction. We can use these strengths to transform some of their weaknesses.

Pictures provide a focused "freeze-frame" of the desired skill or step in the process, and can be extremely helpful to zoom in on specific details, like the setting on the microwave. They can also be helpful for the student to remember specific steps in a sequence. The student can easily pull up a still image in their mind. However, please don't limit yourself to using only pictures. As soon as you've learned how to insert pictures into your Video Stories, inserting video is just as simple. Video provides your student with much more information and connects singular details, actions and ideas into essential concepts.

> "I THINK IN PICTURES. Words are like a second language to me. I translate both spoken and written words into full-color movies, complete with sound, which run like a VCR tape in my head."
>
> -Temple Grandin, Ph.D.
> *Thinking in Pictures*

Video

Zooming In

Video can spotlight the exact skill or lesson being learned and showcase only the important details. Many students have difficulty focusing on the pertinent pieces of information. Their brains may not be able to distinguish what is relevant from what is irrelevant. Or there may just be too much information for the student to process at once. For example, when involved in a social interaction, the

student may be keenly aware of the scent of the person's shampoo rather than her words. Through video we can help these students focus by cutting out all the extraneous distractions of the classroom and zooming in on what is significant.

Acting Out

Video engages the students to become an active part of the learning process. They have to *do* something, and when they do it, they learn it. The student *realizes* the essential concepts by acting them out in authentic real-life situations. There is another benefit of acting it out. When the students do something, something else happens. The video can be edited down to demonstrate the precise moment of cause and effect in which the students' actions result in a pleasant outcome. The student finishes a task and therefore earns free time. The student uses his words to ask for bubbles and receives them. The student shares a toy and enjoys playing with a friend. The video illustrates this cause and effect relationship in an active visual way that the student may never have understood before.

Adding a Script

Students with limited verbal speech or poor articulation sometimes do not realize that words and simple phrases can be extremely helpful to them. Perhaps they have had so many unsuccessful attempts at communicating that it doesn't seem worthwhile. Maybe they have been so confused by social situations that they don't realize there are some unwritten rules to make sense out of social situations. With video as a teaching tool, we can show the students that communication can be reasonable and rewarding.

> "Continuing to link visual cues with written directions helps the child move from a world of only 'thinking in pictures' to one in which the pictures have a sound track, and the child begins to think in words."
>
> - Bryna Siegel, Ph.D.
> *Helping Children with Autism Learn*

With video, it is possible to reenact situations that are important to the individual, "freeze-frame" the parts in which language would be helpful, and add a "soundtrack" to the video, as Byrna Siegel talks about in her wonderful book Helping Children with Autism Learn. It is at this moment of focused connection, that Video Stories can incorporate language to label the people and objects involved in the scenario as well as provide a soundtrack of phrases the student can employ to more easily obtain what he or she wants. Once the students understand that simple words can help them obtain a desired item more effectively, they will begin to use words more and more to express their wants and needs. Video Stories are able to connect language with the benefits of language in a concrete and visual way.

Verbal Communication

With Video Stories, you can incorporate your voice or the student's voice reading the words on the slide or introducing a scene in the movie. Many students who are uninterested or uncooperative when asked to read other material will be extremely motivated to read the words of their own stories and record their voices into the computer. Students with communication devices can get their words ready and then record the entire section. In PowerPoint, you can have the slideshow play this verbal recording automatically or when the student clicks on a microphone icon. You can also make the slideshow highlight each word as it is pronounced. In Windows Movie Maker and iMovie, you can add text and verbal narration as well. Whatever the student needs, the student gets. Remember true communication involves presenting information so the other person can understand.

Teach

Classroom Expectations

The first day of school always fills me with intense excitement and the same amount of dread. Adrenaline is shooting through my veins. My students probably feel the same way. I have 18 students in the same room, all of whom are wound up with summer enthusiasm, many of whom are in a brand new environment and do not know the expectations and routines in my classroom, and none of whom are ready to work. The situation could quickly collapse into chaos.

This year, on the first day, my camera never left my hand. I used it to get the students to demonstrate my classroom rules and expectations. They were eager to show off. I encouraged them to show me how to stay "cool."

My classroom Rules are "Stay Cool: Cool Hands. Cool Feet. Cool Words." I realize these rules are rather vague, but I use my video camera to have my students illustrate exactly what each of the rules would look like. The returning students were ready to show the new kids how to "be cool," and the new kids were eager to show the older kids how "cool" they could be.

We compare staying cool to getting "Hot," which refers to acting angry or mean, and getting "Cold," which means acting whiney or timid. "Staying Cool" means acting calm and confident. We talk about self-esteem and different methods of staying cool. This concept comes from a wonderful video program for adults with special needs called "Be Cool." Several years ago, my students watched the videos and decided they could make their own.

Anyway, the first day was a Success! Each of my students not only learned the rules and followed them, but watched themselves with tremendous pride as they demonstrated the essence of coolness.

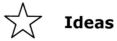 **Ideas**

Your Classroom Rules,
Character Development,
Safe Use of Materials,
Foundations of Friendship,
Hall Pass Procedures,
Work Time/Free Time.

Cool Words

Brian says "I am cool."

Brandon says, "Please read me my book."

When Derek says "Thank you for being my friend," David says "You're welcome."

When the teacher asks for something, Erik says, "OK."

When Zack knocks the sack off the table, he says, "Sorry." Robert says, "Don't worry about it, Zach."

David says, "Ok, I will stay cool and do my work."

Brandon says, "I can laugh, and stay cool."

David says, "We're cool and we're staying cool. We're having work."

Robert says, "I'm cool like superman."

David says, "I'm sorry I got Hot. I'm staying cool now." Derek says, "Don't be sad. I'm here for you." David says, "I'm sorry. I made a mistake."

Zach says, "It's cool to be cool."

Schedules/Routines

Video Stories have been a powerful tool to help my students understand the other visual supports and interventions we've put in place to help them. For instance when we introduce a new reinforcement system, we often confuse the student by explaining all the information verbally. I have found that when I present the information about how to earn rewards or free time in a Video Story, with the student participating in and illustrating the process step by step, the student comprehends the system better and becomes more personally involved with it.

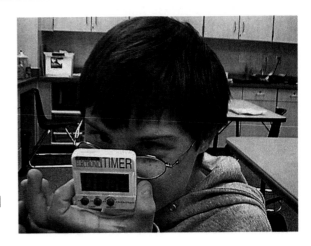

I'd like to give a brief description of how I've set up some visual supports to establish a positive and predictable structure in my classroom. Some of my students have a visual behavior contract and a nickel tower, and Erik demonstrates how they work in the following Video Story. In class, we call them a token chart and a money chart. On the token chart, the student reads "I will stay cool and do my work, I am working for …" The students can choose from about ten different free time activities and place their selection at the end of the sentence. When the students are doing their work or behaving appropriately, the teacher pulls a Velcro token from the back of the chart and places it in one of the four boxes on the front. This gives the students a visual reminder of how long they will need to work before they can earn a reward. After they've earned four tokens, they can have free time for ten minutes. If the student does not stay cool or shows some form of aggression, the teacher removes the icon of the desired free time from the chart and the student loses the opportunity for that desired free time for the rest of the day. Don't worry; they still have nine other choices of free time activities. The students also earn plastic pennies for staying cool, doing their work, sitting in their seat, using their words, etc. These pennies are kept on a Velcro strip at the bottom of the nickel tower. When they get five pennies, they can trade up for a nickel. They can save up their nickels to buy treats and toys from the classroom store. The format of this visual reinforcement system has been wonderfully effective for both increasing on-task behavior, and also learning the value of money, one-to-one correspondence, and counting by fives. Visual supports such as these can be extremely helpful, and Video Stories are a way to further illustrate what they mean to the students.

Many students, especially those with autism, tend to feel much more comfortable when given a general routine or sequence to follow. Video Stories establish a general structure or simple sequence for a situation, which the student can follow step by step. It is possible to provide a general structure or sequence for many of the experiences your student will encounter—social situations, daily routines, and classroom expectations. Even changes to routine can sometimes be given a structure.

I had a student for which fire drills were an extremely traumatic event. I'm sure some of you have run into that problem as well. He would scream and run back into the school or hide. We made a Video Story for him about a fire drill. He acted out how to "stay cool" in a fire drill step-by-step -- cover his ears, walk with the teacher, follow her outside, sit in the grass, talk with his friends, wait, and come back in. We provided essential background information like "It's OK. It's not a real fire." and "We practice so we can be safe." The next time we had a fire drill, he was able to pull up those video clips in his head and act them out. He got through the fire drill with no problems.

We can help students feel more settled and comfortable by offering a predictable routine for any reoccurring event in their life that may be confusing to them, such as a visit to Grandma's house, a stay in a hotel, or a power outage. Even if the routine does not happen entirely as planned, it gives the student a much-needed framework to understand the event.

☆ **Ideas**

Daily Schedules, Routines for Activities, Classroom Management Systems, Free Time Rules, Transitions, Change of Schedule, Change of Teachers, Assemblies, Fire Drills, Power Outages, Field Trips.

How I earn
Free Time
I can do my work and earn
money and free time.

When free time is over, I can
choose a new free time for next
time. I choose Draw.

I bring my free time chart over
to my desk and do my work.

After about five minutes of work,
my teacher gives me a red token.

I am really good at reading. I am
so smart.

When I work hard and follow
directions, my teacher gives me
pennies. When I have 5 pennies,
I trade up for a nickel.

I trade 5 pennies for a nickel.

After I work some more, I get another red token on my chart.

Then I do a little more work and I get a third red token on my chart.

When I'm finished with my work, I get four tokens. 1, 2, 3, 4.

I get a new free time. I set the timer for 10 minutes. When the timer rings, I can start over.

I can choose a new free time.

Appropriate Behavior

Sometimes we come up with a brilliant behavior intervention plan, but then we get stuck because we are trying to explain the plan or teach the replacement behavior verbally and the student is uninterested or unable to understand. Video Stories can be especially helpful to teach replacement behaviors because they show the new behavior step-by-step, demonstrate the wonderful things that will happen when the student performs the behavior, provide a clear explanation of how and why this behavior works, and also

get the student engaged in that behavior right away as they act it out for the video.

A word of caution: Since the student's motivation to imitate the video clips of themselves is so strong, it is best to avoid having the targeted students demonstrate an inappropriate behavior. Try to teach the positive replacement behavior without making an example of the problematic behavior. You can validate the emotion the student feels and teach him appropriate ways to express his emotions, such as "When I feel mad, I can ask for a break." Video Stories rely on the powerful desire of the student to imitate himself in the video, so be sure that the actions and responses of the student in the video are exactly what you'd want to see again.

You may feel the need at times to explain what will happen as a consequence to an inappropriate behavior, in order to instill some impulse control or help the students predict and evaluate the outcome of their actions. For some of my higher-functioning students, it has been very beneficial to predict "what would happen if…" and include those outcomes in their stories. For example, we made a Video Story about how Sara could stay cool, even if a friend was rude to her at lunch. We discussed what would happen if she got "Hot," yelling and threatening her friend. The students in this group were able to think through the situation and realize that Sara might get in trouble with the principal, and would definitely lose her friendship. We also discussed what would happen if she got "Cold" and started pouting or crying. The students concluded that Sara might get made fun of, and the other person may not want to be her friend anymore. Finally we discussed how Sara could handle the situation by staying "Cool." She could take a deep breath, ignore the rude comment, change the subject, or calmly let the friend know that her feelings were hurt. If you're interested in teaching your students how to predict and understand consequences in this way, consider your students carefully and plan a performance that will not inadvertently "glorify" the inappropriate behavior.

I offer the next video story, entitled "You Can't Always Get What you Want," as both an example and a non-example. Some of you may read the following Video Story and think to your self – "Oh, You're not supposed to show the negative behavior!" and you're absolutely right. I learned a little from that mistake. I was trying to show the consequence for throwing a tantrum at the end of free time. I had a model student who usually follows directions act out a little tantrum. The Video Story effectively illustrated the consequence, but still emphasized some unproductive behavior since the other students thought his mock tantrum was funny. If your students would respond in a similar way, I would encourage you to leave the negative behaviors out of the Video Stories whenever possible, or have a peer tutor, puppet, or adult demonstrate it, rather than a student with severe special needs. But I include this story anyway, because it primarily focuses on the positive behavior of saying "OK" and following directions, and it worked amazingly well.

Some of the boys in my class wanted to keep playing after free time was over, imagine that. When the teacher would say, "Free time's over," Erik, who liked to do his own thing and be the center of attention, would often put on a show. He would yell, "No" and then hoard the toys, gathering them to himself. I sometimes tried to gather them up faster than he could, and then carefully pry the remaining toys out of his hands, but I realized he was really enjoying the one-on-one attention, and the fact that all the other kids were watching him. He was giggling and hiding under various desks as if we were playing a game. If we had been playing a game, he would clearly have been the winner. He had escaped the work and received lots of attention from myself and his friends. He had shown he was in control of the situation.

> "Insanity: Doing the same thing over and over and expecting different results."
>
> -Einstein

I feel embarrassed to write about how I participated in his power struggle, but at least I eventually learned that it wasn't working and changed my tune. I guess I'm not completely insane, according to Einstein's definition.

We created a video story about what everybody needed to do when free time was over. We added some goofiness and humor to make it stick. Erik was so motivated to be on video, that when the teacher said, "You need to do your work," he said, "OK!" All the boys said, "OK!" Later, they would ask me to watch the Video Story again and again.

Then, on many different occasions, from that day on, when the teachers would say to Erik, " Time to do your work." Erik said "OK!" I sometimes caught a puzzled glint in his eye, as if he were thinking to himself, "Why in the world did I say OK?" but he would follow through and do what we had asked.

 **Ideas**

Waiting, Walking, Finishing a Task, Listening, "Cool" Hands, Feet and Words, Asking Permission, Dealing with Frustration, Tolerating "No," Saying "OK," Ending Free Time, Transitioning to a New Task, Using Materials Appropriately, Cleaning Up, Personal Hygiene

You can't always get what you want.
Sometimes you have to wait.

One day, Erik and Austin wanted to watch a movie. They said, "I want movie please."

Mrs. Roberts said, "You need to do your work first." This made Austin angry and he threw a little fit.

Uh-Oh, Austin. When you're hot, you lose movie for the rest of the day.

But when the teacher told Erik, "You need to do your work first." Erik said, "O.K."

Later on, Austin wanted to play with a ball. He asked his friends, "Will you play ball with me?" Derek and Erik said, "O.K."

When free time was over, the teacher said, "Now you need to do your work." ALL the boys said, "O.K."

Language Development

Let me tell you another story about one of my students named Brian. Brian is an extremely bright and complicated individual. He has autism and has previously been called "functionally nonverbal" because his speech was very limited and was mostly echolalic, which means he repeats phrases but rarely initiates them. Brian is a comedian, and thrives from the attention he receives, whether positive or negative. Since his speech was so limited, he sought out attention in many inappropriate ways. He would try to get a rise out of teachers and fellow classmates in any way he could. When he saw a reaction, no matter how slight, he would giggle and laugh and continue.

We have created many Video Stories to increase his communication skills in order to help him gain attention in more positive ways. We brainstorm to come up with phrases that we think he might want to say or that might benefit him in certain situations. We record him repeating these phrases and then edit out our verbal prompts, so he sees and hears himself using language successfully and independently. After watching the Video Stories, he begins to initiate the phrases at appropriate times, without any prompts. The stories also help the teachers, parents, and classmates understand his speech successfully, because we become familiar with the language he is using. When he speaks he gets an extraordinary amount of attention. We squeal with excitement, saying things like "I love knowing what you're thinking about," and "You are so funny." Brian giggles from the attention and continues using his words.

He has made amazing progress in his language development, initiating each of the phrases we've made into video clips, and has developed sincere, mutual relationships with us. However, on days that Nichole, my partner teacher, or I are absent, he still gets agitated and reverts to his old methods of getting attention. These shenanigans can set the other kids off and result in a full-blown terrible day. One morning, Nichole had taken a sick day and I had to break the news to Brian. I could see his body start to get agitated. His breathing was shallow; his hands were twitching.

One of Brian's specific interests is sickness, so I knew that all Brian wanted to do was concentrate on Nichole and the fact that she was sick. Asking Brian to concentrate on something else at this point would undoubtedly lead to a Trouble. Now I have a "nonverbal" kid who wants to talk. Why not?

We made a video "Get Well" card for Nichole. I prompted Brian to say the things I knew he would want to say to her, and then edited those prompts out, so the Video Story shows him saying it independently. It is really one of the most precious get well cards I have ever seen, if I do say so myself. I'd encourage you to visit the website and watch the "Nichole's Sick" Video Story, just for its heart-melting capabilities. In his incredibly cute and intentionally comical way, Brian says things like, "I know, Poor Thing," "I miss you," and "Get back here!" He loved to see himself in the videos and initiated those phrases throughout the day, without any mischief-making, because he was able to gain attention and express his frustration with words. Each time he remembered that Nichole was gone, rather than scream or throw something, he could say, "Poor thing, Tummy hurts." or "Nichole, Stay in bed!" and express his feelings successfully.

We've made several Video Stories like this to increase his language development. Once he sees himself and hears himself saying things that are cute, comical, or elicit positive attention, he begins to initiate the phrases right away. We've used what we know about his interests and his personality to guess what might be most motivating and useful for him to communicate. In the next section on social skills, I explain how we've used Video Stories to teach him to initiate greetings and interact with his classmates in appropriate ways and thereby make dramatic and life-changing improvements in his abilities to make and keep friends.

Whatever phrase, question, or comment the student would benefit from knowing how to say, you can teach with Video Stories. If the student is truly nonverbal and unable to articulate or repeat words and phrases, make the worthwhile effort to increase the student's ability to communicate with their communication device or Picture Exchange Communication System (PECS). Whatever mode of communication the student has can be used in the Video Stories, and when they see themselves communicating successfully in their Video Stories, they will likely be motivated to initiate more communicative attempts and increase their responses.

Talking on the phone is another important language development skill. Many students, who could otherwise get their point across or show that they understand in face-to-face conversation, get lost when talking on the phone. We can teach this skill, because when you think carefully about it, there are some essential phrases that help us carry out successful phone conversations every day. A sweet little student named Micah called me the other day and really surprised me with her language skills on the phone. During the course of the call, she used some very helpful phrases, such as "Just a minute," "What was that?" "Let me write that down." "Could you spell it for me?" "Well, I'll let you go now." I was struck by how beneficial those little phrases are and how simple it would be to teach those phrases with video stories. You could have a student call another student (using a cell phone or a phone in a different room) and record both of their responses. The students would likely be thrilled to talk on the phone, and you could record several different conversations to help maintain flexibility.

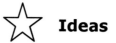 **Ideas**

I Want, I Feel, I Need,
I Like, I See, I Hear,
Questions & Answers,
Comments, Greetings,
Goodbyes, Before & After,
Expanding Sentences,
Adding Details, Articulation,
Phone Calls, Concepts from
Speech Therapy

Nichole's Sick.

Poor Nichole

Your tummy hurts. Ow!

I know…Poor Thing.

How Sad!

Whew! No Fun!

Poor Honey.

I am cool.

I'm doing my work.

I miss you.

Get Better Soon.

Stay in Bed.

Drink your water.

Take your medicine.

& Get Back Here.

Social Skills

Simple communication can be explicitly taught to make social interactions more effective and rewarding. For example, one student in my class with very limited communication and social skills would grab, drag or poke other students when he wanted to play. This was not an effective way to make or keep friends. Once I understood the function behind this behavior, I made a Video Story about inviting friends to play. In the story, I taught a short phrase, "Want to play?" I modeled the use of the phrase, and

provided verbal and written prompts. I filmed the student's attempts and included the correct ones in his Video Story, editing out any prompting. He quickly made the connection that this simple phrase resulted in a much more pleasurable playtime, and began using his new communication skill right away.

Our little comedian, Brian, also wanted desperately to interact with his classmates, but didn't have the language or social skills to do this successfully. We made a Video Story for him in which we prompted him to initiate greetings with his friends. We edited out our verbal prompts, so Brian watched himself talk to his friends independently. He said short phrases like, "Hey You," "What's up, Buddy?" and "Give me five." It was thrilling to see Brian begin to initiate these phrases on his own. Now he is able to do it all the time.

Video Stories also give the student the opportunity to focus on his or her individual needs, independent of other students. For students with autism and other challenges, the confusion and frustration of social demands in the classroom can lead to withdrawal or inappropriate behavior. Even the need for social skills can be addressed without the stress of a room full of students. The student can practice his desired skill one on one with his favorite classmate or with a teacher.

Video Stories can also be a good way to increase a student's tolerance for group settings. If the student is capable of watching a movie with other students, possibly one of the easiest group tasks, then that student can be successful watching his Video Story with others. This can be a great way to begin to use the targeted social skills. It may start with one relatively approachable, non-threatening student sitting by him as he reads through his stories. At each point in which the opportunity to rehearse a skill presents itself, the student can show off his new skill to the friend. The friend of course should respond with just the right kind of praise to reinforce the skill. When this has become a successful and pleasant experience, you can gradually increase the number of students participating and introduce the other students' slideshows.

We have also focused on recognizing and responding to emotions, teaching appropriate ways to handle frustration, confusion, and anger. Staying cool in the midst of these emotions is an invaluable life skill.

One of my students would habitually fall to pieces anytime he felt confused or frustrated. He had become almost entirely dependent on prompting from an adult, and refused to use his own brains to solve a problem or think through a situation. If a classmate looked at him funny, or if a teacher didn't give him the answer, he would burst into melodramatic tears. In several of the video stories, we gave him the role of the cool, confident problem solver. It was very interesting to see his view of himself change as he watched the movies. One day, shortly after these Video Stories were made, he saw that I was frustrated about something, and he said to me, "Stay Cool. Take a deep breath. You can handle this."

 **Ideas**

Greetings, Goodbyes, Initiating Conversation, Asking Questions, Apologizing, Ending Conversations, Manners, Taking Turns, Personal Space, Asking Permission, Understanding and Responding to Emotions, Making Compromises, Correcting, Complimenting

Friends have Fun Together

Playing, Making Good Deals, and Taking Turns.

Erik wanted someone to play with. He asked Brandon, "Want to Play?" Brandon said, "Sure, I'll play." Whoo Hoo!.

Brandon said, "What can we play?" Robert said, "Let's play bubbles."

Jenn said, "I want to play ball." Now they've got a problem. Robert wants bubbles and Jenn wants the ball. What should they do?

Erik said, "Uh-Oh! What are we going to do?"

Brandon knew how to stay cool. He said to himself, "Take a deep breath. I'm OK. I'm Cool. I can handle this."

Brandon had a plan. He knew how to make a good deal. A good deal means each person feels good. He said, "Bubbles first, then ball. OK?" Erik said, "OK."

Robert blew bubbles.

Then Erik asked him, "Can I have a turn?" Robert said, "Your turn, buddy."

Later Jenn said, "I want a turn." Erik handed it to her. He said, "Here you go, Jennie. Come on. Get the ball. You can do it. Yeah! Got it!"

Erik had fun playing ball with Jenn. It is fun to play with your friends, take turns, and make good deals when you can so that everybody has a fabulous time.

Independent Living Skills

Video Stories are the perfect way to teach independent living skills and any behavior that is necessary to participate in the community, because they distill complex sequences of events into easy accessible steps that the student can remember. You will also be able to print out the PowerPoint and each slide will remind the student visually of the steps.

We have a classroom store where my students sell treats and drinks to the other students and teachers in the school. We found an old cash register from the thrift store, and it proved to be a wonderful motivator for learning to count money. Even if you don't have the opportunity to have a school-wide store, you could use a cash register in your classroom to create Video Stories about many different purchasing and selling situations.

We've also made Video Stories about important food safety and personal hygiene information to keep the students healthy. We called it "Fight Bac: Bacteria can make you Sick," based on the wonderful website www.fooddetectives.com, which has great music videos and interactive games to teach food safety. Our video story demonstrated how to stay healthy by putting leftover food in the refrigerator, washing hands, dishes, countertops and utensils correctly, cooking foods to the right temperatures, and separating raw and ready-to-eat foods.

You can create Video Stories to teach essential life skills, such as using the microwave or stove, preparing simple recipes, and cleaning up afterwards. The camera can zoom in for specific details and help the students remember.

It takes many different skills to find and keep a job in the community. You could develop these skills by making Video Stories about searching for jobs, filling out job applications, setting the alarm clock and arriving on time, completing the specific job requirements, speaking politely to coworkers and customers, solving problems or disputes, reading the schedule, calling in sick, depositing your check, and saving money.

Your students may need to be instructed in other community-based skills, such as using the library, reading the bus schedule, following a map, and recognizing community signs. Procedures for how to find safe help in the community would also be extremely helpful.

 **Ideas**

Purchasing/Selling,
Making Appointments,
Serving & Preparing Food,
Kitchen Safety, Job Safety,
Nutrition, Healthy Lifestyles
Paying Bills, Budgeting
Providing Personal Info,
Stranger Danger,
Driving or Bus Safety,
Taking Directions.

Uh-Oh! It's a Fire Drill.

Beep. Beep. Beep.
Oh, great! Uh-Oh. It's a Fire Drill.

It's SOOO Loud.
I cover my ears.

It's OK. We're Safe.

We practice so we can be safe.

Safe means nothing can hurt us.

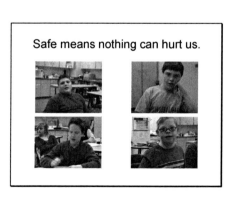

It is NOT a REAL fire.
We're just practicing.

I'll find the teacher.
There you are.

We walk with the Teacher in the hall. We have Walking Feet so we don't fall.

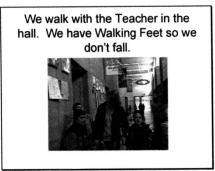

We have Walking Feet out the door. We wait for the Teacher to tell us more.

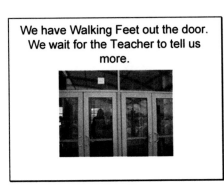

We walk with the Teacher to the street. When she says Stop, we freeze our feet.

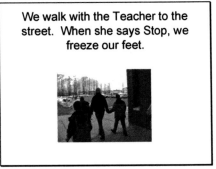

We look to the left and to the right to see if there are any cars in sight.

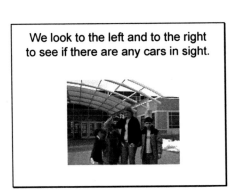

If there are no cars, we cross the street. We stay with the teacher and have walking feet.

We have a place to sit on the curb.

I talk to my friends.

I wait.

After a while, my teacher will say "We can walk back in now. It's OK." If I stay with my teacher & have walking feet, I will get free time or a special treat.

Academic Content

Some students are so bright, and so capable, but have a terrible time focusing on academic material. They could understand and remember the complex material if they were somehow engaged with the material. This was the case with several students who I was supporting in the general education science class. We had a wonderful teacher who encouraged each student to "show what they know" in their own creative way. I asked my students if they'd like to make a video PowerPoint together to teach the class the concept of density. It was like I had flipped a switch to "On" with these students. All of a sudden, they were eager to learn and I had their undivided attention.

The students decided to base their video on the educational television show "Bill Nye, the Science Guy." They wanted to conduct an experiment to figure out which was more dense, Coke or Diet Coke. They added their own intense creativity and unique personalities. In order to perform in the videos, they needed to understand what they were doing and saying. I had a captive audience. We wrote the script on the board. I showed them how to measure mass, volume, and density. They mastered the material quickly and completely. Then, when they presented the video PowerPoint to the science class, they were able to teach their fellow classmates.

Video Stories can engage the students with the academic material they need to learn, and expand their understanding. If the students are learning about weather, they could demonstrate their knowledge with a weather forecast. If they are learning about civil rights, they could make a news broadcast. If they are learning about division, they could act out a word problem. They could write and perform plays in English class and film the

production. They could learn a lot about responsibility and job skills by filming a documentary about what goes on behind the scenes in the lunchroom or the office.

Literacy can be expanded by using Video Stories as a supplement to the reading program, especially for those students who are less than excited about reading and writing. I have mentioned before that students who refused to read their regular material were eager to read, write, and record their own Video Stories. Here's another idea: In my class, after reading a children's story, I took pictures of the picture on each page, zooming in with my camera. Then , in order to save time, I asked a peer tutor to insert each picture onto a PowerPoint page. The students rewrote the story in their own words by explaining what was happening in each picture. This exercise helped to develop listening comprehension, recalling details, sequencing events, and writing complete and descriptive sentences.

PowerPoint Paragraphs are another reason to learn how to use PowerPoint. Students increase their writing skills by creating sophisticated PowerPoint presentations. My students write PowerPoint paragraphs about the topic of their choice for their writing assignments, or science or social studies projects. Each of these PowerPoint Paragraphs includes a recording of the students reading their words. My students, without exception, have been more motivated to write on the computer than on paper. They can create a much more presentable and even professional quality product in very little time.

The student's opportunity to write and express themselves shouldn't be limited to the words they can spell. They have more ideas and thoughts in their heads than "cat," "dog," and "mom." In order to facilitate the student's expression, some of my students dictate their sentences to a peer tutor or a teacher, and then type the sentences into PowerPoint from a written model. Other students only ask for assistance on tricky words. When they need help, a peer tutor or teacher writes the word or words on a whiteboard or paper by their computer. Then, it's time for the editing process. Many of my students have learned to right click on words that are underlined in red or green, and choose the correct spelling or grammar. They need a minimum of one complete and correct sentence on each slide. Then they can record their own voice and insert pictures and animation. I have set a rule of only one picture and only one animation per page, because students who want to insert lots of pictures and animations will just need to create lots of complete correct sentences on other pages.

When the students record their voice, they increase their fluency. The first time, they may stumble through the words. The second time, they may read the words correctly, but without much feeling or emotion. They listen again and try again, until they get it just right. The verbal component of the slideshows increases their fluency and their comprehension of the written words. When the students present it to the class, they can read it out loud, click on their voice recording, or choose another student to read it. You can upload the PowerPoint paragraph slideshows to your classroom website or blog, so your students are able to share them with their friends and family. Visit my website or blog to see my students' PowerPoint Paragraphs. Click on "Orion Magazine."

It's possible that as you begin to think about ways to use Video Stories in your classroom, you may discover some hidden creativity in yourself, your aides, and your students. As you provide more opportunities for your students to create, they may surprise you with their inherent or increasing imagination and resourcefulness. For example, Garrett, the scientist in the Video Story about density, gave us quite a shock when he showed us a movie script he had written during his free time for his classmates to perform. It was a spoof of the Wizard of Oz, filled with appropriate humor, great dialogue and amazing character development. Previously, when asked to write about appointed topics in his English class, both Garrett and his teachers were frustrated and disappointed. But now, given the opportunity to write a movie script, Garrett astonished us with his original ideas and writing skills. As a class, we acted out and filmed the movie. Though I had intended it as a Reader's Theater, most of the students memorized their parts. We presented the movie at the end of the year party for parents and peer tutors. Thanks to an impressive outflow of creativity from my students and teacher's aides, the show was a success. Garrett even wrote a 176 page comic book version of the movie, and sold many copies at the party. He shattered our pre-conceived notions of what students with autism can and cannot do, and helped us to see his true talents.

 **Ideas**

Consider how an academic skill could be applied or demonstrated in real life situations and then have the students act it out.

**Bryan
The Smartest Guy**

Science Rules!

Density is the # of particles
smushed into 1 space.

Density= Love

Step 1: GET MASS!

Step 2: GET VOLUME!

Diet Coke= .95g/ml Coke= .98g/ml

Diet Coke is less dense. It floats.

Coke is more dense. It sinks.

It's a Scientific Breakthrough!

Create

In my classroom I have faced exhaustion, heartache, and struggle trying to help students with autism and other challenges, but I have also experienced many life-changing Success Stories. I have seen students who were withdrawn, defiant, and even aggressive begin to open up, laugh, communicate, and do much more than anyone thought they could do through the process of becoming "movie stars."

I am confident that each and every child has a fascinating and miraculous potential to grow – to face challenges and learn from them, to rise above seemingly insurmountable obstacles and experience profound and limitless possibility. By growth, I am referring to a kinesthetic experience of sincere, dramatic, positive change. Through the process of creating Video Stories, I hope you will inspire and be inspired by that fascinating and miraculous growth in your own children and students.

Now it's your turn to create your own Success Stories. Uncover the hope that you have for your students. Take the first step toward making your dreams for them a reality.

The rest of the book is meant to be read in front of your computer as you create.

You can do it!

"If you lose hope,
somehow you lose the vitality
that keeps life moving,
you lose that courage to be,
that quality that helps you go on
in spite of it all.
And so today I still
have a dream."

— Martin Luther King, Jr.

To Capture:

Your camera/camcorder will come with detailed instructions that will be tailored specifically to your camera. Your camera company will also have extensive tech support online and by phone. I encourage you to use this support when you run into problems. So rather than provide vague instructions for all cameras or specific instructions for one kind of camera, I will let you know what you might need to connect your camera to your computer and set it up to capture and edit your video clips using Windows Movie Maker or iMovie.

To Capture Pictures:

Your camera will either have a USB cable to send pictures to your computer or it will have a memory card. The memory card can be inserted directly into some newer computers or you can purchase a port that you can connect your memory card to your computer. Your camera will also come with a driver disk. A driver disk is a CD program that you will need to install onto your computer to enable your computer to recognize the camera. Once your computer recognizes your camera you can send or copy and paste your pictures into a folder in "My Pictures." It is best to keep these photos organized as you go along. If your photos involve more than one student, you can name the folder after the Success Story you are creating.

To Capture Video:

Some cameras now are allowing you to store and send short video clips through USB (or Flash Drive), but many camcorders require a Fire Wire cable to send video from the camera to the computer. There are two types of Fire Wire – 4 pin and 6 pin. The smaller one in the picture is 4 pin. Take a look at your camcorder and your computer to see which kind you will need to buy. If your computer doesn't have a jack that looks like either of these, then you may need to get it installed.

File Formats and Camera Compatibility

If you're on the lookout for a new camera, you will find many new options to choose from. There are tape-based devices that record the video to mini digital video cassettes; these are called DV or HDV camcorders. Several new cameras are tapeless devices and either store the video files in clips on the USB (Flash) device or directly in DVD format. I would suggest you stay away from camcorders that only save in DVD format, because you are not able to edit them at all. Be sure to ask lots of questions. Ask what mode and file format the video is saved in.

When you're capturing video on a Windows Computer in Windows Movie Maker, the video will automatically be saved as .WMV, unless you change the format in the <u>Other Settings</u> section of the capture process. Windows Movie Maker and PowerPoint 2003 and 2007 will play .WMV files. When you're capturing video on a Mac computer using iMovie, the video will be saved as a .MOV format. PowerPoint 2004 or 2008 for Mac will play the .MOV file format.

There are a multitude of video file formats out there. You can tell the format by the three or four letters after the period at the end of the file name. Some people have run into obstacles because their videos were saved in a file format that is not compatible with the programs on their computer. If this is the case, you have two options: you could either switch to the programs that would work with the file, or you could convert the file formats by downloading a video converter. I have been researching video converters for several months. I have not found any free ones that consistently convert correctly, but I can recommend the Agile converter, which you can purchase online and download for $29 at www.avsofts.com. Though each video conversion program will operate a little differently, they are basically very simple. You will need to <u>Add </u>or <u>Import</u> your video file, choose the <u>Profile</u> or <u>File Format</u> that you want, and then press <u>Start</u>.

Deciding Which Program to Use

You can decide whether to use Windows Movie Maker (or iMovie for Mac Users) or PowerPoint to create your Video Stories (Mac Users can use PowerPoint for Mac). Eventually you will probably want to learn to use both Movie Maker and PowerPoint, because they are very beneficial to teaching. Both programs have their merits. Movie Maker is easier to transfer because it's a single video file rather than a video embedded in another program. You can even email a video story if it is made within Movie Maker. A video story made in Movie Maker will play through automatically like a real movie. PowerPoint Video Stories offer a slower pace slide show which is really helpful if you want your students to read through each page and then watch their movie. The decision comes down to whatever is best for your students.

I've listed some characteristics of each program to start you thinking.

Windows Movie Maker or iMovie	**PowerPoint**
o Easily Transferrable	o Runs at your own Pace
o Saved as Movie File	o More Room for Text
o Can be Emailed	o Students can Read words and then watch the Video
o Runs Automatically like a Movie	o Students' peers are learning to use PowerPoint
o Can be made into a DVD	o Can Add Animations
o May Run More Smoothly	o Shared by CD or USB
o Shared by Email, CD, DVD, or USB	

Mac Users: If you are using a Mac computer, you will want to capture your videos in iMovie and then either create the Video Story in iMovie or PowerPoint for Mac. Though the pictures in the PowerPoint section may look a little different than your screen, the directions should be transferrable to PowerPoint for Mac. PowerPoint 2004 for Mac will correlate to the instructions for PowerPoint 2003 in this guidebook, and PowerPoint 2008 for Mac will correlate to the PowerPoint 2007 instructions.

Now you're ready to begin your Video Story!

How To Create Video Stories in Windows Movie Maker

To Open Windows Movie Maker:

Click on <u>Start</u> > <u>Programs</u> > <u>Windows Movie Maker</u>.

In this section, each button that you need to click will be <u>underlined</u>, and each sequence of clicks will be shown with a ">" between them.

To Capture Video clips in Windows Movie Maker:

Make sure your camera is On, set to "Play" or "Computer" mode, and the Fire Wire or Flash drive is connected properly. Click on <u>Capture from video device</u>.

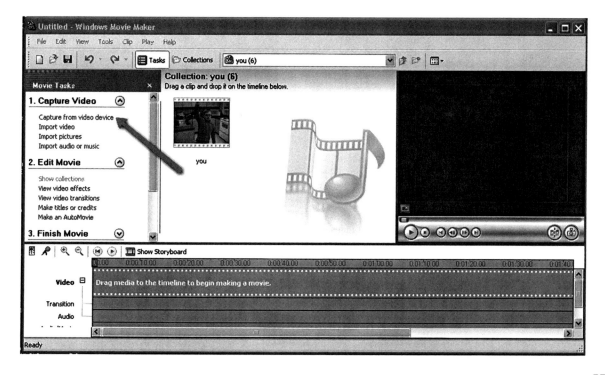

Choose a name for your movie based on the main topic of your Success Story. To stay organized, you can use the same name for each video in a success story with a different number at the end. For Example, if the story concept was about trying something difficult, you could entitle the video clip"YouTry1" and then "YouTry2." It is best not to put any spaces, symbols or periods in your title. Click <u>Next</u>.

Choose <u>Best Quality for Playback on My Computer</u> > <u>Next</u> > Select <u>Capture parts of the tape manually</u> and <u>Show preview during capture</u> > <u>Next</u>. You could also click on Other Settings and choose a different file format if you wish.

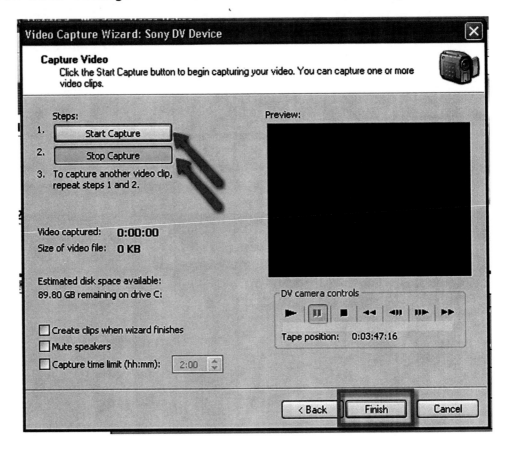

Now, though it make take some time to get used to, the process is really rather simple. You will press on the play icon to watch your video tape. (Press Rewind and Fast Forward while it is still playing, rather than stopped, because it goes so quickly.) When you are ready to capture a video clip, press <u>Start Capture</u>. When you are done, press <u>Stop Capture</u>. Then <u>Finish</u>. You can click on the video clip to watch it on your computer. The videos will be automatically saved into "My Videos" on your computer. To find them, open <u>My Documents</u> then <u>My Videos</u>. Now that you've captured your video, you're ready to create a video story! You can choose to create it within Movie Maker or in PowerPoint.

To Create a Video Story Within Windows Movie Maker:

To Import Videos:

Click on <u>Import Video</u> > Browse for the video you want by clicking the <u>Down Arrow</u> and looking in <u>My Videos</u>. Click on the <u>Video</u> you want > <u>Import</u>.

You can also look for previously imported videos by clicking the <u>Down Arrow</u> next to Collections.

Drag the <u>Video</u> from the collection to the timeline.

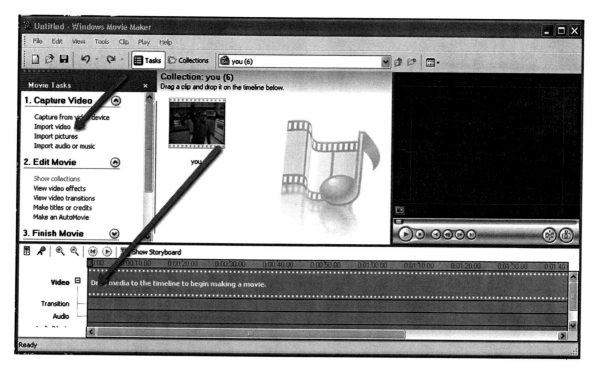

To Understand the Timeline:

This is the place to combine your videos with words and audio. You can increase the size by clicking the "Zoom In" button or you can drag the blue line that separates the collection workspace from the timeline a little higher.

There is a blue marker that runs vertically through the movie. You can drag the Blue Marker to skim through the video and stop at the place you want to view the movie.

To Import Audio or Music into Windows Movie maker:

Click Import Audio or Music > Browse by clicking the Down Arrow to find the Song you want from My Music > Import. Click on the icon of the Song and drag it down to the timeline.

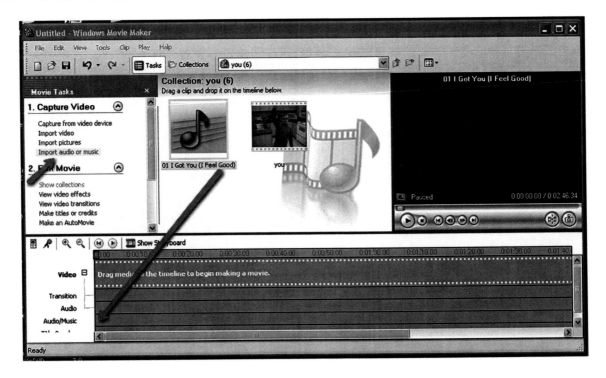

To Rip Music (Transfer music from the CD to your computer):

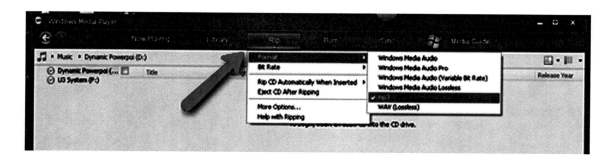

Put the CD in the computer, if an automatic screen comes up, Choose <u>Rip Music from CD</u> > <u>OK</u>. If the screen doesn't come up, Open Windows Media Player by clicking <u>Start</u> > <u>Programs </u>> <u>Windows Media Player</u>.

Put a check by the songs that you want to rip. Click on the <u>Down Arrow </u>under <u>Rip</u> > <u>Format</u> > <u>MP3</u>. <u>Rip Down Arrow</u> > Click on <u>Song</u> > <u>OK</u>.

To Adjust the Audio levels:

Click <u>Tools</u> > <u>Audio Levels</u> > Slide the <u>Marker</u> towards either the Audio Clip or the Video Clip.

Here's another way. On the timeline, Click on the <u>Audio Clip</u> or the <u>Video Clip</u> that you want to adjust > <u>Clip</u> > <u>Audio</u> > Choose from <u>Mute</u>, <u>Fade In</u>, <u>Fade Out</u> or <u>Volume</u>.

To Add Words to your Video Story:

Windows Movie Maker has a variety of ways to add text to your story. You can add titles at the beginning of the movie, captions on the clips, pages of text before or after the clip, and credits at the end. It really is quite fun. Try it, you'll like it. Click on <u>Make Titles or Credits</u>.

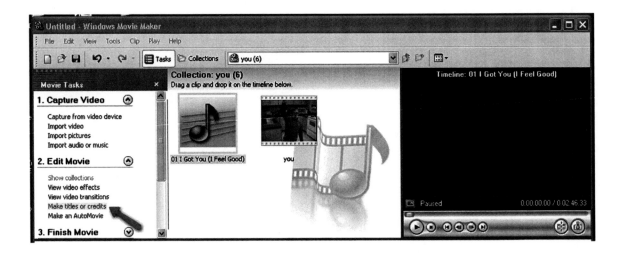

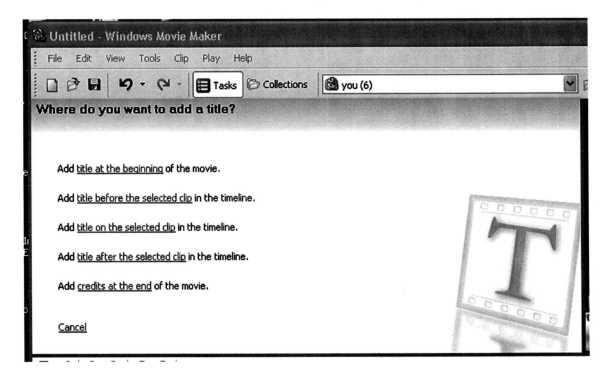

The title screen appears. Choose whether you'd like to put your words at the beginning of the movie, before your selected clip, on the clip, after the clip, or at the end. Click on the Title Option you want.

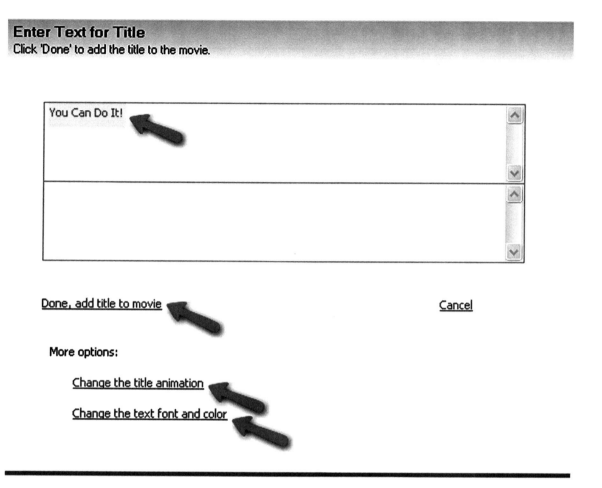

Enter your text. Click <u>Change the Title Animation</u>. Browse through the many options and click on the <u>Animation</u> you like. If you'd like, you can also click on <u>Change the Text Font and Color</u>. You will be able to preview your Title Animation in the monitor window. Then, click <u>Done, Add Title to Movie</u>.

To adjust the duration of the title, click on the <u>Title Overlay</u> in the timeline and drag it longer or shorter.

If you decide you want to change the animation or font again, right-click on the <u>Title Overlay</u> > <u>Edit Title</u>.

To Trim Video or Audio Clips:

You can trim out any unwanted footage at the beginning or end of a clip. Hold your mouse at the beginning or end of a Clip until a Two-Way Arrow appears. Click and Drag to trim either side of the Clip.

It helps me to look at the audio levels underneath the video clip to get an idea of when something was said so I can trim before or after it.

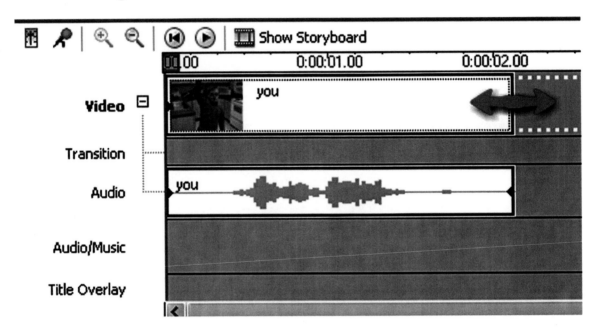

To Edit Out Parts from the Middle of a Clip:

Click on the Video Clip in the timeline to select it. In the monitor window, Press Play, and then Pause just before the unwanted portion. Click the Split button, which is at the bottom right corner of the monitor window. This will split the clip into two parts. Press Play again and then Pause just after the unwanted part. Click the Split button. Now click on the separate Clip of the unwanted portion in the timeline, and press Delete.

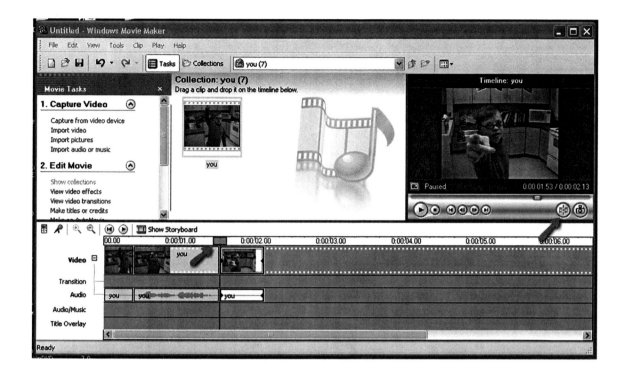

To Save Your Work:

There are two different ways to save your Video Story in Windows Movie Maker. Saving it as a project will allow you to make changes to it later. Saving it as a movie won't let you alter it afterwards. I would suggest you save it as a project first before saving it as a movie, just in case.

To Save Your Work as a Project:

Click <u>File</u> > <u>Save Project As</u> > Find the correct location to save your Project file by clicking on the <u>Down Arrow</u> next to "Save In" > Type your Project name > <u>Save</u>.

To Save Your Work as a Movie:

Click <u>File</u> > <u>Save Movie File</u> > <u>My Computer</u> >Type a Name and Choose Location by clicking the <u>Down Arrow</u> next to "Save In" > <u>Best Quality for Playback on my Computer</u> > <u>Save</u>.

If you'd like a higher quality video, click <u>Show More Choices</u> rather than "Best Quality for Playback on my Computer" > <u>Other Settings</u> > <u>Video for LAN - 768 Kbps</u> > <u>Save</u>.

For Extra Help:

Check out the video tutorials on my website – www.wsdstaff.net/~jroberts. Click on <u>Success Story Instructions</u>.

Or go to www.microsoft.com/windowsxp/using/moviemaker.

How To Create Video Stories in PowerPoint 2003:

To Open:

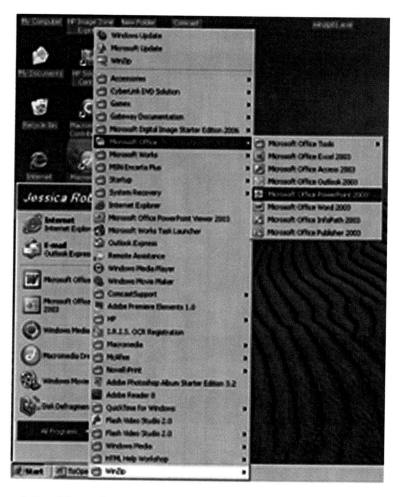

In this section, each button that you need to click will be <u>underlined</u>, and each sequence of clicks will be shown with a ">" between them.

Double Click on <u>PowerPoint</u> Icon on your desktop. OR

Click <u>Start</u> > <u>Programs</u> > <u>Microsoft Office</u> > <u>PowerPoint</u>. To make it easier next time, you can right click on Microsoft Office PowerPoint in the programs menu and choose <u>Create Shortcut</u>.

Take a few minutes to explore. Hover your mouse over some of the picture icons and a written description will appear to explain what that button can do. This guide will go into great detail to make sure you understand how to use each function, but in the spirit of learning you should take some time to play, discover, and create.

To Choose a Layout:

PowerPoint opens to a title page. If you want a different layout, click <u>Format</u> > <u>Slide Layout</u>. This is just like scrap-booking. Choose a layout from the right side and double click on it. It is not really necessary to choose one specifically suited for picture or movie, but it might help you feel organized.

If you want to move a text box around, click on the <u>Box</u> (slanted lines will appear) and hover your cursor over the edge until a 4-pointed arrow appears. Click and Drag the <u>Box</u> to desired place.

To delete a box, click on the <u>Box</u> twice and press <u>Delete.</u>

68

To choose your own Background:

Students who have trouble focusing may benefit from plain black text on white background. However, as you get students involved in creating their own slideshows, the first exciting thing they will want to do is change the color of the background and words. So here's how to do it.

To make a solid color background, click <u>Format</u> > Background > <u>Down Arrow</u> > <u>More Colors</u> > (Choose a color) > <u>OK</u>.

To make a two color background, click <u>Format</u> > Background > <u>Down Arrow</u> > <u>Fill Effects</u> > <u>Two Colors</u> > <u>Down Arrow</u> > Choose each <u>Color</u> and <u>Shading Style</u> at the bottom > <u>OK</u> > <u>Apply to All</u>.

To use a preset background, click <u>Format</u> > <u>Background</u> > <u>Down Arrow</u> > <u>Fill Effects</u> > <u>Preset</u> > Choose <u>Color</u> and <u>Shading Style</u> at bottom > <u>OK</u> > <u>Apply to All</u>.

To Make Your Picture the Background:

Click <u>Format</u> > Background > <u>Down Arrow</u> > <u>Fill Effects</u> > <u>Picture</u> > <u>Select Picture</u> > Choose the <u>Picture</u> from your files > <u>Insert</u> > <u>OK</u> > <u>Apply</u>.

To choose a fancy sophisticated background design, click <u>Format</u> > <u>Slide Design</u> > Choose a <u>Design</u> from right side of screen.

To Insert Text:

Click on a <u>Text Box</u>. Slanted lines will appear to show that you've selected it. Type in it. TADA! Easy.

To move the box, click on the <u>Box</u>, then hover your mouse over the edge until a four-cornered arrow appears. Click and Drag the <u>Box</u> to where you want it.

To add a text box, click on the <u>Text Box</u> button on the bottom toolbar. It looks like a newspaper with an "A" in the corner. Then Click and Drag to make it the size you'd like.

To delete a box, click it twice and press <u>Delete</u>.

To change the font or size of the text, use the toolbar at the top of the screen.

To change the color of the text, click on the <u>Arrow</u> next to the "A" on the toolbar at the top.

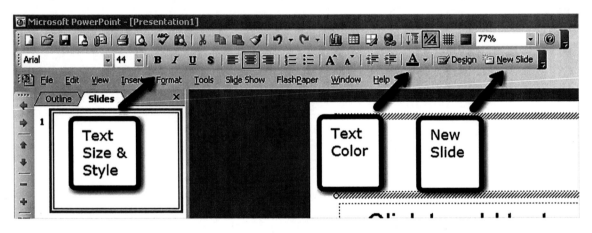

To make your words fancy, check out the <u>Word Art</u> button on the bottom toolbar. It looks like a sideways blue "A." Select a style. Click <u>OK</u>. Then type your words and click <u>OK</u>.

To insert speech bubbles like those in comic books, click <u>AutoShapes</u> then <u>Call Outs</u>, then click and drag where you want it on the screen.

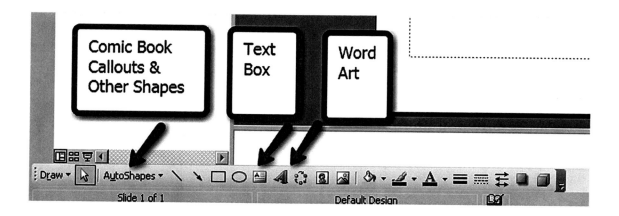

To Insert Pictures:

Click <u>Insert</u> > <u>Picture</u> > <u>From File</u>. Choose a <u>Picture</u> from your files. Click <u>Insert</u>. If picture is too large, find a corner and Click and Drag it till it's the desired size.

To Insert a New Slide:

A slide is like a page in your PowerPoint story. Click <u>NewSlide</u> on the top toolbar. OR Click <u>Insert</u> > <u>New Slide</u>. You can move back and forth between the slides by clicking on them in the toolbar on the left side of the screen.

To Insert Clip Art:

Click <u>Insert</u> > <u>Picture</u> > <u>Clip Art</u>. On the right side of the screen a Clip Art box will appear. You can type in a keyword and press <u>Go</u>. If they don't have what you're looking for, check on <u>Clip Art on Office Online</u>.

To Use Pictures from the Internet:

My students love to get pictures from the internet to use in their PowerPoint Paragraphs. You can right-click on the picture and choose Copy, then Paste it into your PowerPoint Slide. OR You can right-click on the Picture and choose Save Picture As. That way you can save it in My Pictures and use it as a background for your slide. (See Background Instructions.) Copyright laws allow you to use pictures for educational not-for-profit purposes.

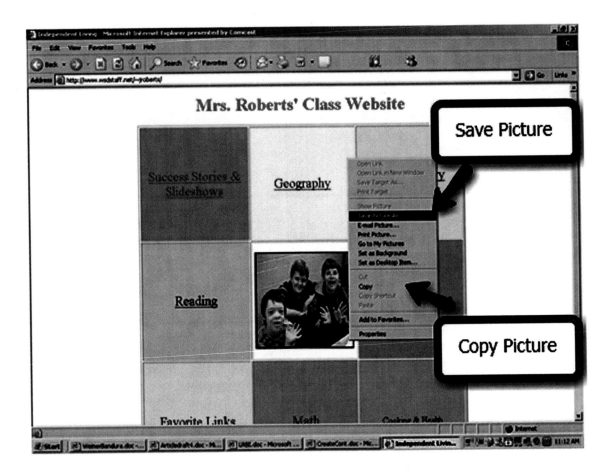

To Insert Audio:

Click Insert > Movies and Sounds > Record Sound. You might need to press the down arrow to see Record Sound. Insert the microphone. Click Record (red circle). Stop (blue square). OK. An icon speaker will appear in the PowerPoint. You can Click and Drag it to move it or make it larger.

To improve sound quality: Double click the speaker button on the bottom tool bar to see if the microphone is activated. If not, click on <u>Options</u> > <u>Properties</u> > Check <u>Microphone</u> > <u>OK</u>.

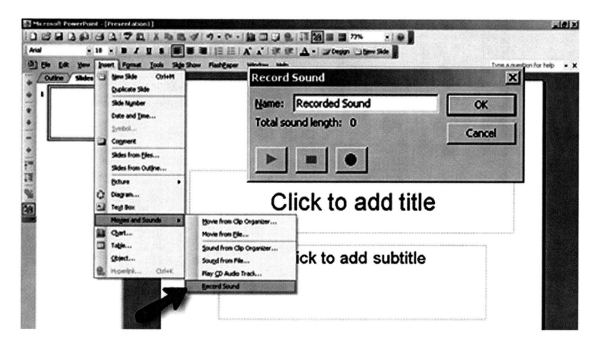

To Insert Video:

Capture and edit movies first with Window Movie Maker. The video clips will be saved to My Videos in My Documents.

To Insert Video: Click <u>Insert</u> > <u>Movies and Sounds</u> > <u>Movie from File</u>. Choose the <u>Movie</u>. Click <u>OK</u>. A pop-up box will appear, asking you how you want to start the movie. Choose <u>When Clicked</u> or <u>Automatically</u>.

To make the video zoom to full screen: Right-click on <u>Edit Movie Object</u>. Under Movie Options, check <u>Zoom to Full Screen</u> and Press <u>OK</u>.

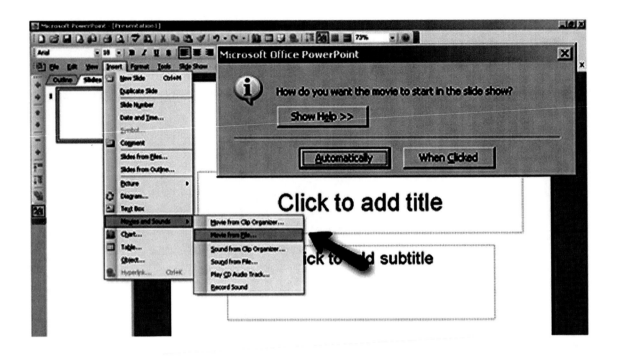

To Create Animation:

Click <u>Slideshow</u> > <u>Custom Animation.</u>

Highlight the <u>Words</u> or select the <u>Picture</u> that you want to animate. Click <u>Add Effect</u>. Choose from <u>Entrance</u>, <u>Emphasis</u>, <u>Exit</u>, or <u>Motion Path</u>. Select an <u>Effect</u>. You many click on an effect to see it previewed. (Or press <u>Play</u> at the bottom)

You may adjust the starting time, direction, or speed of the effect.

To remove the effect, click on the <u>Down Arrow</u> by the animation and click <u>Remove</u>. (Or select the <u>Animation</u> and click <u>Delete</u>.)

To add sound effects to an animation, select the <u>Animation</u> and click on the <u>Down Arrow</u> > <u>Effect Options</u>. Click on the <u>Down Arrow</u> next to sound. Select a <u>Sound Effect</u> and press <u>OK</u>. You can also animate the text by word or by letter under the Effect Options Tab.

To Play a Slide Show:

Click on <u>Slide Show</u> > <u>View Show</u>.

To Create Transitions between Slides:

Click Slide Show > Slide Transition. Choose a Transition. (At the end of the list is Random Transition.) You may change the speed of transition or add a sound effect. Choose whether to advance through the slides on a mouse click or automatically after a certain amount of seconds. Click Apply to All Slides.

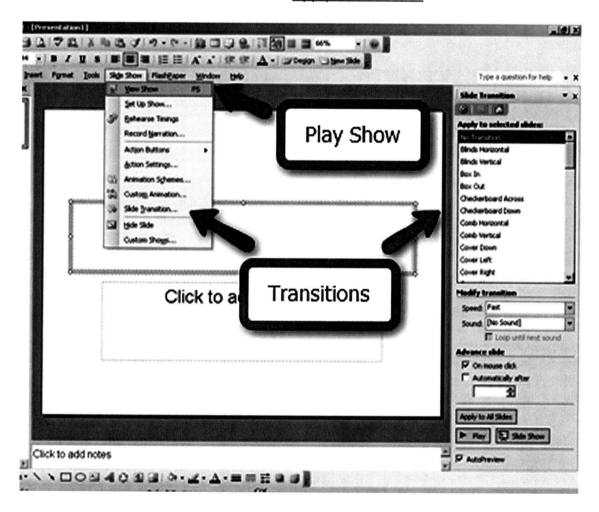

To exit a Slide Show:

To exit a slideshow press esc.

To Save:

As you're working on it, you may save it in the regular way (File > Save As > Choose Location and Name > Save). However, since you've added pictures, sounds, and/or videos, you will NEED to package your slideshow once you're finished to keep all the files together and be able to transfer your slideshow to other computers.

To Package the Slideshow:

This means wrapping up all the files together so the computer can find them later. It is very important. Think of it as wrapping up a package with all the fun stuff inside.

Click File > Package for CD. (Sometimes this is called Pack and Go or Wrap for CD.) Type in a name for the File. Click Options. Make sure all the boxes are checked. The PowerPoint Viewer means that your students will be able to view it at home even if they don't have the PowerPoint program at home. Copy to Folder. Browse. To "Browse" means to look through you computer for the right place to save your file. Choose the placement of your PowerPoint file. Click Select > OK.

If you're going to put the Video Story on the internet, you'll need to add a password for security reasons. You can add a password as you're packaging the slideshow. Click File > Package for CD > Type in name for file > Options> Type in a password that your students can remember in the blank. You'll want them to be able to access it. Click OK > Confirm Password > OK.

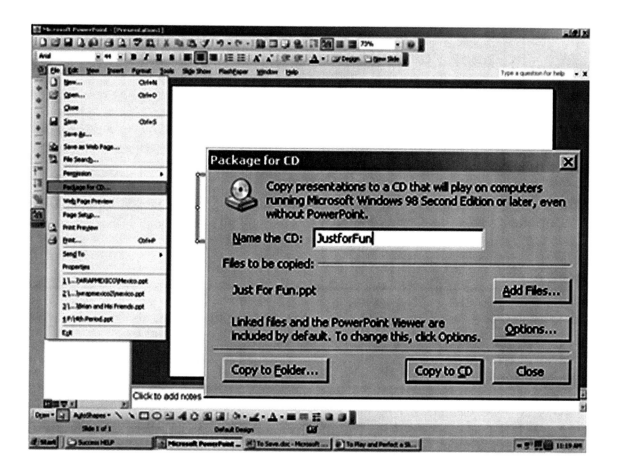

To Save Packaged PowerPoint to a USB:

PowerPoint files that include video and pictures are too large to be saved to a Floppy Disk. You will need a USB Memory Stick to transfer your slideshows around. These are inexpensive and sold at any office store. If you are saving to the USB Device, Follow the directions for "Packaging the Slideshow." After checking the boxes on the Options page, click <u>Copy to Folder</u> > <u>Browse</u>. Look for <u>Removable Disk</u> or <u>USB Memory Device</u> in the Browser. Click <u>Select</u> > <u>OK</u>.

When you're finished, make sure to eject the USB Memory Stick safely by pressing the button on the bottom toolbar that has a green arrow on top of a USB Memory stick. Click <u>Safely Remove USB Mass Storage Device</u>. Wait for a "Safe to Remove USB Mass Storage Device" message.

To Save Packaged PowerPoint to a CD:

Copying your students' video stories to CDs is a great way to share their success with their parents. This is another important part of generalizing the skill. The parents will begin to refer to the language used in the Success Story and the skill will be applied in various settings around the community. It's easy and inexpensive to copy it to a CD. You will need a CD-R Drive and a blank CD-R.

Follow the instructions for "Packaging the Slideshow." After checking the boxes on the Options page, click Copy to CD.

To Print:

Simply click File > Print. Under the heading "Print what:" you can choose from Slides, Handouts, Notes or Outline. Then click OK.

For Extra Help:

Check out the video tutorials on my website – www.wsdstaff.net/~jroberts. Click on Success Story Instructions.

Or Go to http://office.microsoft.com/en-us/powerpoint and click on the PowerPoint 2003 Demos under the training section on the left side of the screen.

How To Create Video Stories
in PowerPoint 2007

To Open PowerPoint 2007:

In this section, each button that you need to click will be <u>underlined</u>, and each sequence of clicks will be shown with a ">" between them.

Double click on the <u>PowerPoint</u> icon on your desktop. OR Click on <u>Start</u> > <u>Programs</u> > <u>Microsoft Office</u> > <u>Microsoft Office PowerPoint</u>.

Take a few minutes to explore. Click on the Home, Insert, and Slideshow tabs at the top and see what options you have under each category. Check out the Microsoft Icon (four squares) in the top left corner. This guide will go into detail to make sure you understand how to use each function, but in the spirit of learning you should take some time to play, discover, and create. This new version of PowerPoint is laid out a little differently, but once you learn how to find each part, you might like its layout a little better. Think of each of the tabs (Home, Insert, Page Layout...) as a little well-organized closet. In the closet you'll find pictures on each button to describe what the button can do. If you hold your mouse over the button, words will appear to explain what the button's purpose.

To Open an Existing PowerPoint:

Click on the <u>Microsoft Icon</u> (Four boxes in top left corner) > <u>Open</u> > Choose the correct location by clicking on the <u>Down Arrow</u> next to the "Look In" section > Choose the <u>PowerPoint</u> file you want to open > <u>Open</u>. (A PowerPoint file will have a PowerPoint icon or ".ppt" at the end of the file name.)

To Change the Layout:

This is a lot like scrapbooking. You put the boxes where you want them. This step is for you to stay neat and organized. You can also double click on a box and press delete to erase it or click in the middle of a box and drag it to move it to a new place.

To change the layout, Click on the <u>Home</u> Tab > Click on <u>Layout</u> > Choose your favorite layout.

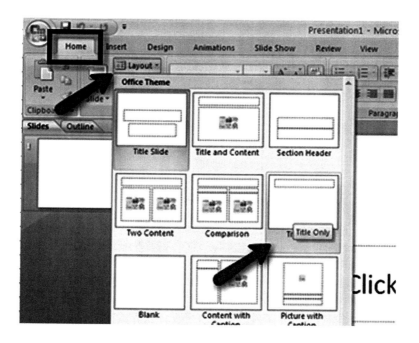

To Make a New Slide:

A Slide is like a page of the PowerPoint. Click on the <u>Home</u> tab on the toolbar > <u>New Slide</u>. You can click back and forth on your slides in the toolbar on the left of the screen. You could also drag slides to a new sequence in the slideshow.

To Write in the PowerPoint:

Click on a <u>Text Box</u> and start typing.

To Insert a Text Box:

Click on Insert > Text Box. Then you'll click on your slide, hold your mouse button down, drag it diagonally across the screen, and let go. Click on the Text Box to write in it. You can click any of the formatting buttons under the home tab to adjust the way your text looks. You can click on the white circles on the corner or sides of the box and drag it to make it larger or smaller.

To Insert a Shape:

Click Insert > Shapes > Choose a Shape. You can put words on the shape by putting a text box on top of it. You can insert comic book style speech bubbles which are called "Call Outs" under the shape category.

If you double-click on the text box or shape or click on the Drawing Tools Format tab that appears at the top of your screen, you can even add Word Art, Shadows, Background Color, and Outlines to your text box or other shape.

To Change the Background:

Students who have difficulty focusing may benefit from plain black text on white background. However, as you get students involved in creating their own slideshows, the first exciting thing they will want to do is change the color of the background and words. So here's how to do it.

Right-click on a blank space on your slide > Choose Format Background. This screen will appear with lots of options. Play around a little to figure out what each button can do. Change the Color of the background by clicking on the <u>Down Arrow</u> by the Paint Can Icon. Add your own Picture as the background by Clicking on <u>Picture or Texture Fill</u> and choosing the picture from your file. Change the Transparency of the Background by sliding the <u>marker</u> next to Transparency. Click <u>Apply</u> to make the change to the current slide OR Click <u>Apply to All</u>.

To Insert a Picture:

Click the <u>Insert</u> tab > <u>Picture</u> > Choose your <u>Picture</u> from My Pictures > <u>Insert</u>.

If the picture is too big, drag your mouse to the corner of the picture until the cursor changes from four-arrows to two-arrows, Click and Drag it in. Then you can click on the middle of the picture and drag it to where you want it.

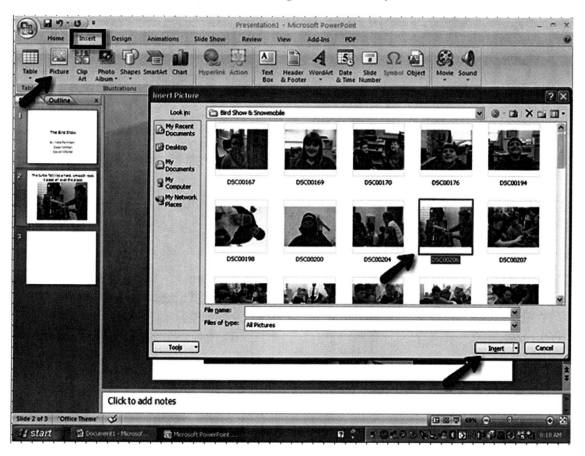

To Insert Clip Art:

Click <u>Insert</u> > <u>Clip Art</u> > Type a general keyword under "Search" on the right side of your screen > <u>Go</u> > Click on the <u>Clip Art</u> you want. You can Click and Drag a corner to make it bigger. To move the clip art, click on the center and drag it to the position you want.

To Insert a Transition between Slides:

Click on <u>Animations</u> > Choose a <u>Transition</u> or scroll down to the end of the Transition list and choose the <u>Question Mark</u> (Random Transition) > <u>Apply to All</u>.

To Make the Slideshow Run Automatically:

Click <u>Animations</u> > Under the Advance Slide Category check <u>Automatically</u> and enter the <u>Number of Seconds</u> > <u>Apply to All</u>.

To Insert a Movie:

Click on the <u>Insert</u> tab > <u>Movie</u> > Choose <u>Movie</u> from My Videos > <u>OK</u>. If you want it to start when you click the mouse, click <u>When Clicked</u>. If you want the video to start automatically, you click <u>Start Automatically</u>.

To Insert a Sound:

Click on <u>Insert</u> Tab > <u>Sound</u> > <u>Record Sound</u>.

Plug the microphone into the jack that has a picture of a microphone on it. Double click on speaker volume, to check that a microphone is activated. (If not, click <u>Properties</u>, <u>Recording</u>, <u>Microphone</u>.) Press the <u>Record</u> button. Speak with your mouth a couple inches away from the microphone. Then, press <u>Stop</u>. Press <u>Play</u> to listen to the recording. If you like it, click <u>OK</u>. If you need to fix something, click <u>Cancel</u> and start the process over. I usually have my students try several times until their reading is fluent and their voice is filled with some sense of confidence.

To Insert a Song:

Click <u>Insert</u> > <u>Sound</u> > <u>Sound from File</u> > Look for the <u>Song</u> in My Music > <u>OK</u>. Choose <u>Automatically</u>.

To make it keep playing across several slides, click on the <u>Song</u> (speaker icon) > <u>Animations</u> > <u>Down Arrow</u> by Animate > <u>Play across Slides</u>. OR Click on <u>Song</u> > <u>Animations</u> > <u>Custom Animation</u> > <u>Down Arrow</u> by the Animation on the right side of screen > <u>Effect Options</u> > Start <u>From Beginning</u> > Enter the Slide Number you want the Song to Stop After > <u>OK</u>.

To Create Animation:

Highlight the <u>Picture</u> or <u>Text</u> that you want to animate. Click <u>Animations</u> > <u>Custom Animation</u> > <u>Add Effect</u> > Choose from <u>Entrance</u>, <u>Emphasis</u>, <u>Exit</u>, or <u>Motion Path</u> > Select an <u>Effect</u>. You can click on the <u>Down Arrow</u> next to your Animation to adjust the Timing, add a Sound Effect, or remove your Animation.

To Play a Slide Show:

Click on <u>Slide Show</u> > <u>From Beginning</u>.

To Save a PowerPoint:

Since your PowerPoint includes pictures and/or video, you will need to save it differently to make sure all the files are linked together. Think of it as wrapping up a package with all the fun stuff inside. This step is called packaging. Once you have packaged your files together, you can choose to save the PowerPoint to a location on your computer, to a USB Memory Stick, or burn it to a CD.

To Package Your PowerPoint:

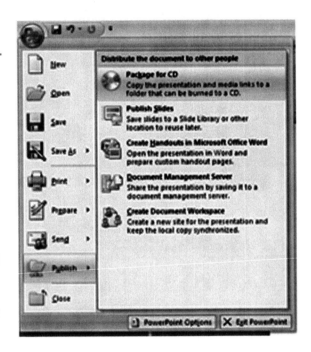

Click on the <u>Microsoft Icon</u> (Four squares in top left corner) > <u>Publish</u> > <u>Package for CD</u>. The "Package for CD" screen will come up. You can name your file in the blank by "Name the CD." Then click on the "<u>Options</u>" tab on the right side. Make sure the "Viewer Package" is checked, as well as "Linked Files," And "Embedded True Type Fonts." If you wanted to add a password to your PowerPoint for security on the internet, you can add a password now. Click <u>OK</u>. Then you may choose to <u>Copy to CD</u> if you have a CD burner on your computer OR you may choose <u>Copy to Folder</u>.

To Save Packaged PowerPoint to Folder:

Click "<u>Copy to Folder</u>" > Browse > Click on the <u>Down Arrow</u> next to the "Look In" section > Choose the right <u>Location</u> to put the file > <u>Select</u> > <u>OK</u>.

To Save Packaged PowerPoint to a CD:

Insert a blank CD, click on <u>Copy to CD</u> > If it asks you to link files, click <u>OK</u>.

To Save Packaged PowerPoint to a USB or Flash Drive:

Click on <u>Copy to Folder</u> > <u>Browse</u> > Click on the <u>Down Arrow</u> next to the "Look In" section > Choose the <u>USB drive</u> (This drive may have different names, such as "Removable Disk" or "USB Memory Device.") > <u>Select</u> > <u>OK</u>.

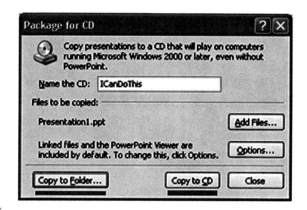

To Save in order to Play in PowerPoint 2003:

PowerPoint 2007 Slideshows have new technology and need to be saved differently in order to be played on a computer that has PowerPoint 2003. However, PowerPoint 2007 is able to open and play PowerPoints made with the 2003 version. When playing a 2003 PowerPoint in 2007, it helps to click the <u>Microsoft Icon</u> (Four squares in top left corner) > <u>Convert</u>.

To save a 2007 PowerPoint to play on a computer with 2003, click on the <u>Microsoft Icon</u> > <u>Save As</u> > <u>PowerPoint 97- 2003 Presentation</u> > Choose correct location by clicking the <u>Down Arrow</u> > Save. Then Package the PowerPoint and Save to a Folder, USB, or CD.

To Email a PowerPoint:

PowerPoints with video clips are too big to be emailed. However, smaller PowerPoints with just pictures can be emailed by clicking on the <u>Microsoft Icon</u> (Four Squares in top left corner) > <u>Send</u> > <u>Email</u>. This will open up your default email account. If that doesn't work, open up your email account, create a new email, click <u>Attachments</u> (Sometimes this looks like a paperclip.) > <u>Browse</u> to find for your <u>PowerPoint file</u> > <u>Attach</u> > <u>Send</u> Email.

To Print a PowerPoint:

Click on the <u>Microsoft Icon</u> (Four Squares in top left corner) > <u>Print</u> > Choose to print each Slide or a Handout > <u>OK</u>.

For Extra Help:

Check out the video tutorials at my website – www.wsdstaff.net/~jroberts. Click on <u>Success Story Instructions</u>.

Or go to http://office.microsoft.com/en-us/powerpoint and click on the <u>PowerPoint 2007 Demos</u> under the Training Section on the left side of the screen.

How To Create Video Stories in Apple iMovie 08

To Open iMovie:

Click on <u>Finder</u> > <u>Applications</u> > <u>iMovie</u>. This will transfer iMovie to your dock. Double click <u>iMovie</u> from the dock.

> In this section, each button that you need to click will be <u>underlined</u>, and each sequence of clicks will be shown with a ">" between them.

To Capture Video to your Computer

New Project...	⌘N
New Folder...	
Duplicate Project	
Project Properties...	⌘J
Move Project to Trash	⌘⌫
Merge Events	
Split Event Before Selected Clip	
Move Rejected Clips to Trash	
Space Saver...	
Import from Camera...	⌘I
Import iMovie HD Project...	
Import Movies...	
Page Setup...	⇧⌘P
Print Project...	⌘P

In iMovie Click <u>File</u> > <u>Import from Camera</u>.

You can choose between automatic or manual capture in the lower left corner. I prefer manual, because I can capture and edit at the same time and it saves storage space on the computer. However, iMovie makes it so easy to edit once the video clips are on your computer, that you may want to choose automatic.

Click <u>Automatic</u> and iMovie will rewind and capture clips from entire video tape.   OR

Click <u>Manual</u>. Use the play, forward, and rewind buttons to find the part you want to capture. Click <u>Import</u> when you're ready and then <u>Stop</u> when you're done.

The video clips will be saved to your computer under an event name that you specify.

To Create a Video Story in iMovie:

To Import Movies:

When you open iMovie, it will automatically begin a new movie project. Click on the <u>Default Name</u> in the project window and type the name of your Video Story.

You can choose an <u>Event</u> from the event library or Click <u>File</u> > <u>Import Movies</u>.

You can move your mouse over the clips in the event library at the bottom of the screen to preview and decide which clips you will use in your story. This is called Skimming. You can press the <u>Space Bar</u> to play the video and <u>Space Bar</u> again to stop the playback.

You can click on a <u>Video Clip</u> in the event library to select it, and then Click and Drag it to a blank space in the project window.

You can also select only a portion of the video clip by clicking and dragging your mouse over the part of the video you want. Then click on the <u>Selection</u>, and Click and Drag it to the project window.

Once your clips are in the project window, you can rearrange the order by Clicking and Dragging your clips to the desired location.

To Trim your Video Clips:

Choose a portion of a clip, by Clicking and Dragging within the clip to select the part you want. Then, click Edit > Trim to Selection.   OR

Click on the Clip Duration Button that is located in the lower left corner of the clip. Click and drag the Border of the clip at the beginning or end to trim either edge. Then, click Done.

To Play the Movie:

You can skim through the video clips by moving your mouse over the clip (either in the project window or event library). To start playing from a particular point, skim to that point and press the Space Bar to play. Press the Space Bar again to stop.

To watch your entire movie, click on the Play Select Project from the Beginning or Play Select Project Full Screen buttons, which are located at the bottom left corner of the project window. To exit out of full screen mode, click Esc.

To Add Music or Sound Effects:

Click on the Music and Sound Effects Button on the right side of the middle toolbar.   It has an icon of musical notes. You will be able to choose from any of your iTunes or the audio files that come automatically with the program. Double click to preview the song.

To add a song to your Video Story, click once on the Song to select it and then click and drag to the empty black space in your project window.

The song will appear as a green background in the project window. If you need to adjust the volume, click once on the Song and then click on the Adjust Audio button in the center of the middle toolbar. Slide the Volume marker and click Done. If your song is longer than your movie, it will automatically fade out at the end.

You can add a sound effect in much the same way, except instead of dragging it to the empty space in the project window, you will drag the Sound Effect to the exact place on the video clip where you want the sound effect to start. The sound effect will appear as a purple marker on the video clip. You can adjust the duration by clicking once on the Sound Effect marker, and then dragging the Edge. To adjust the volume, click once on the purple marker to select the

<u>Sound Effect</u>, and then click the <u>Audio Effects</u> button in the center of the middle toolbar to make your adjustments.

To Add Voice Narration:

Click on the <u>Voiceover</u> button in the center of the middle toolbar. Click whether you are using a built-in microphone or an external microphone. You'll want to preview the microphone audio levels by speaking into the microphone and adjusting the volume level to as high as possible without going into the red zone. Make sure the Noise Reduction marker all the way to the right and Select <u>Voice Enhancement</u>.

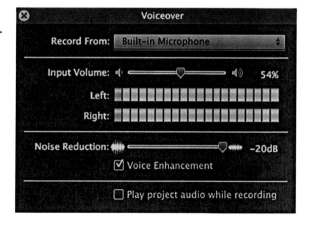

Click on the <u>Video Clip</u> at the point that you want to begin the narration. iMovie automatically gives you a countdown and begins recording. Click the <u>Space Bar</u> to stop. Close the Voiceover window when you're done by clicking on the <u>X</u> in the top left corner.

To Add Words to your Video Story:

Click on the <u>Titles</u> (T) button on the right side of the middle toolbar. Select a <u>Title Style</u>. Then, Click and Drag it to the appropriate place on your video clip in the project window. As you drag it there, you will be able to choose whether you want the title at the beginning of the clip, the end of the clip, or throughout the entire clip. In the viewer window, click on the <u>Title</u> and Type in your words. If you don't want a subtitle, delete the default subtitle text. You can adjust the style and size of the text, by clicking on <u>Show Fonts</u> in the top left corner of the viewer window. You can adjust the placement or duration of the title by Clicking and Dragging the edges of the title marker in the project window.

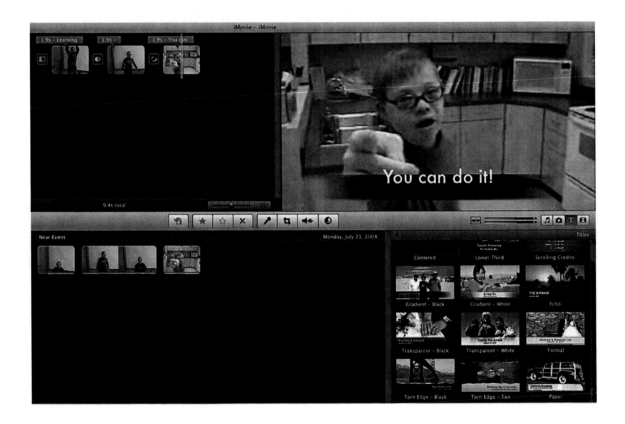

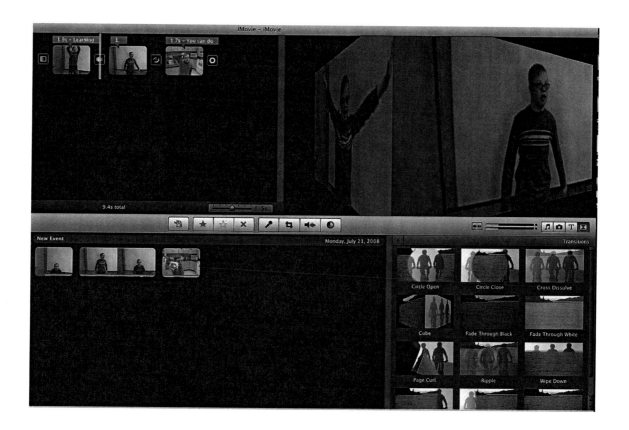

To Add Transitions:

Click on the <u>Transitions</u> button on the right side of the middle toolbar. Select a <u>Transition</u> and Drag it in between the video clips in the project window.

To Save and Share your Video Story:

iMovie automatically saves every change you make. You can share the video files by emailing them, copying them to a CD, creating a DVD in iDVD, or by publishing them directly to your Mac Moble Me Gallery website. You will need to set up your web account at www.me.com. Click <u>Share</u> > <u>Mobile Me Gallery</u>. You can set up a password by clicking <u>Viewable By</u>. Then, click <u>Publish</u> > <u>OK</u>.

For Extra Help:

Check out the wonderful video tutorials at www.apple.com/ilife/tutorials.

Acknowledgements:

My Students

Most important special thanks to my students. I have learned more from you than anyone else. Thank you for allowing me to see how truly amazing you are. I feel lucky to know you and be your friend. Each one of you has changed my life.

Of my students in this guide, some names have been changed and all have provided parental consent to have their photographs and videos shared.

My Students' Parents

Your gentle patience, your search for solutions to the students' challenges, your encouragement of me and your excitement over your childrens' successes have taught me so much. Thank you.

My Wonderful Husband, Ben Roberts

Your constant encouragement, brilliant ideas, and genuine love have inspired me to do more than I ever thought possible. Without you, none of this could have happened. Thank You.

& Many, Many Others

Special thanks to so many people whose insight and ideas, encouragement and helpfulness have made this a Success Story.

Thank You

Nichole Warren-Doman
Ann Miller, Ph.D.
Laura Johnston
Cathy Longstroth
Jocelyn Taylor
Carol Anderson
Trent Bills
Linda Wiggill
Mary Harames
Nora Barker
Josette Nay
MaryAnn Hardy
Laurin Hubbard
Sarah Cox
Steve Elsnab
Art Hansen
Brittanie Stumpp
Sara Woody

Paul & Janiece Swets
Ethel Swets
Christina Graff-Charbonneau
Mary Schaffner
Julie & Mike Nicholas
Susan Burns
Susan Haggedorn
Anne Gompert
Mona Oversteg
Janice Hill
Cindy Quercia
Mary Lamont
Jodie McKnight
Kathy & Craig Johnson
Clara Walters
Jack Mayhew, Ph.D.
Kristin Hadley, Ph.D.
Becky Jo McShane, Ph.D.

Louise Moulding, Ph.D.
Marla Bailey
Missy & Burke Stone
Kyle Hansen
Tom Johnson
Michelle Pyper
Amy Peters
Chelsea Wheeler-Whitby
Mary Jo & George LaTulippe
Cindy Myers
Colby Colvin
Vicky Napper, Ph.D.
Garrett Nicholas
Nina & Randy Wahlquist
Laurie & Mike Foley
Claudia Eliason, Ph.D.
All my Amazing Peer Tutors
All my Loving Family

Cody Johnson
Linda Harrop
Justin McFarland
Derek Nicholas
James Shaw
Daniel Wahlquist
Lynn Raymond
Jeff Marchant
Andrea Harris
Isaac Foley
Tammy Haws
Paul Dykman
Micah Stone
Keith & Candy Colvin
All my Wonderful Secretaries
All my Brilliant Computer Techs
All my Dear Friends
Thank You

Recommended Readings

Baker, J. (2001). *The social skills picture book: Teaching play, emotion, and communication skills to children with autism.* Arlington, TX: Future Horizons, Inc.

Baker, J. E., & Myles, B. S. (2003). *Social skills training: For children and adolescents with Asperger Syndrome and social-communication problems.* Shawnee Mission, KA: Autism Asperger Publishing Company

Coucouvanis, J. (2005). *Super skills: A social skills group program for children with asperger syndrome, high-functioning autism and relted challenges.* Shawnee Mission, KA: Autism Asperger Publishing Company.

Grandin, T. (1995). *Thinking in pictures: And other reports from my life with autism.* New York: Doubleday.

Grandin, T., & Barron, S. (2005). *Unwritten rules of social relationships: Decoding social mysteries through the unique perspectives of autism.* Arlington, TX: Future Horizons, Inc.

Gray, C. A. (2000). *The new social story book:* Arlington, TX: Future Horizons.

Greenspan, S. I., & Wilder, S. (2006). *Engaging autism: Using the floortime approach to help children relate, communicate, and think.* Cambridge, MA: Capo Press.

Siegel, B. (2003). *Helping children with autism learn: Treatment approaches for parents and professionals.* New York: Oxford University Press.

For more information on these books and other updated lists of recommended readings, visit my Shelfari Bookshelf on my blog at www.teacherslittlehelper.blogspot.com or www.shelfari.com/teacherslittlehelper/shelf.

References

Baker, J. (2001). *The social skills picture book: Teaching play, emotion, and communication skills to children with autism.* Arlington, TX: Future Horizons, Inc.

Barry, L. M., & Burlew, S. B. (2004). Using social stories to teach choice and play skills to children with autism. *Focus on autism and Other Developmental Disabilities, 19*(1), 45-51.

Bellini, S., & Akullian, J. (2007). A meta-analysis of video modeling and video self-modeling interventions for children and adolescents with autism disorders. *Exceptional Children, 73,* 254-287.

Buggey, T. (2005). Video self-modeling applications with children with autism spectrum disorder in a small private school. *Focus on Autism and Other Developmental Disabilities, 20*(1), 52-63.
disorders. *Exceptional Children, 73,* 254-287.

Corbett, B. A. (2003). Video modeling: A window into the world of autism. *The Behavior Analyst Today, 4*(3), 88-96.

Coucouvanis, J. (2005). *Super skills: A social skills group program for children with asperger syndrome, high-functioning autism and relted challenges.* Shawnee Mission, KA: Autism Asperger Publishing Company.

Crozier, S., & Tincani, M. J. (2005). Using a modified social story to decrease disruptive behavior of a child with autism. *Focus on Autism and Other Developmental Disabilities, 20(3),* 150-157.

Grandin, T. (1995). *Thinking in pictures: And other reports from my life with autism.* New York: Doubleday.

Gray, C. A. (2000). *The new social story book:* Arlington, TX: Future Horizons.

Sansosti, F. J., Powell-Smith, K. A., Kincaid, D. (2004). A research synthesis of social story interventions for children with autism spectrum disorders. *Focus on Autism and Other Developmental Disabilities 19*(4), 194-204.

Siegel, B. (2003). *Helping children with autism learn: Treatment approaches for parents and professionals.* New York: Oxford University Press.

Soenksen, D., & Alper, S. (2006). Teaching a young child to appropriately gain attention of peers using a social story intervention. *Focus on Autism and Other Developmental Disabilities, 21*(1), 36-44

Wert, B. Y., & Neisworth, J. T. (2003). Effects of video self-modeling on spontaneous requesting in children with autism. *Journal of Positive Behavior Interventions, 5*(1), 30-34.

Jessica Roberts is a Special Education Teacher in Weber School District. She has developed this Success Stories guidebook as part of a Masters Degree in Education at Weber State University. She is deeply committed to her students' success. In her classroom, Jessica designs technology to visually support the instructional material and engage her students in the learning process. She creates personalized video stories which incorporate video clips of the students performing a skill along with the essential information to understand that skill. She has used these multimedia presentations to turn many behavioral, social, and academic problems into Success Stories.

Outside of the classroom, Jessica enjoys spending time cooking with friends and hiking in the mountains of Utah with her husband and two dogs. She is in the process of adopting a child from Thailand.

For More Information

To watch Success Story Examples,

Video Tutorials at each step of creating a Success Story,

More Recommended Readings,

& Technological Updates,

Visit www.wsdstaff.net/~jroberts

& Go to "Success Story Instructions."

The Success Story Examples are password protected.

The password is "Success."

Please feel free to Share Your Successes or Ask Questions

at www.teacherslittlehelper.blogspot.com

or http://blog.weber.k12.ut.us/jroberts.

You may email me at jroberts@weber.k12.ut.us

Made in the USA